Missing Kylie

A Father's Search for Meaning in Tragedy

Books by Mark Myers

Non-Fiction

Missing Kylie

Fiction

Virgil Creech Takes a Swipe at Redemption

Virgil Creech Sings for His Supper

Virgil Creech Rides a Pig

A Concise History of Portsong

Missing Kylie

A Father's Search for Meaning in Tragedy

Mark Myers

Text Copyright © 2016 Mark Myers
ISBN # **978-1530360277**

Cover layout and design: Hassan Hijazi
Cover photo: Cindi Fortmann
Back cover photos: Mike Gillette & Jennifer Style

With special thanks to Robin, Kendall, Jenna, and Meredith Myers for
their letters to Kylie and their inexplicable love of the author.

Dedication

This book and everything I do for the rest of my life is dedicated to my beautiful daughter, Kylie, who fought her battle with a smile and such joy that I am forever changed.

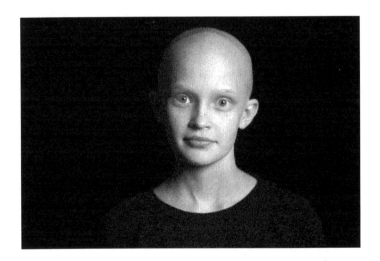

Kylie Elise Myers

Feb 24, 2002 – Feb 13, 2015

Proceeds from the sale of this book will be used to fight childhood cancer in memory of Kylie.

Preface

All of my life I wanted to write a book. I love the power of a story – how a good story can pull you inside a world of fiction and steal your mind for as long as the words flow. Ten years ago, I decided to leave my mundane job to become a celebrated author. Being cautious, I kept my employment while rising at 5 a.m. to carve the masterpiece that would be my legacy. Ironically, it is a coming of age novel about a boy dealing with love, loss, and cancer. When I finished, I sat back and smiled contentedly while I waited for the fame and fortune my novel would bring.

I still have that same job. The book? Well, its printing was limited to one copy that sits on my bookshelf. I've written four more books since – three published with fairly good reviews and just enough sales to pay for themselves. The hours spent writing and learning to create the social media footprint necessary to market my work looks like time wasted to the average man. But I don't believe the average man weaves our stories together – I believe God does.

Who else would write a story where a man devoid of sentimentality has four daughters? Only God with his supremely satirical pen. Our fourth girl was a huge surprise, but she completed our family perfectly. From her earliest days we called her Smiley Kylie because a smile was never far from her face. On April 9, 2014, the pain of a cancer diagnosis put that smile on hold. After she digested the news, she simply said, "God must have a really big, great plan for me." Kylie drew strength from family and immediately wanted her sisters around her. I went home and circled them on the floor in the den to tell them the devastating news. As we held each other there on the floor, I said, "We're going to cry, we're going to pray, then we are going to be smiley for Kylie when she can't."

By the time we got to the hospital, "Smiley for Kylie" was born. Her sisters and I hatched a plan to get friends and family to send Kylie smiles to encourage her. To do so, we needed to set up a website, along with Twitter, Facebook, and Instagram accounts. Not coincidentally, I knew exactly how to do all of that because God had prepared me through my writing experience. In a matter of minutes, Smiley for Kylie had a complete social media presence. What happened next only God could have done! Word leaked out and Kylie got smiles from every state and from all over the world. Celebrities, athletes, politicians, and Broadway stars smiled for her and helped her through her darkest hours. It was incredible.

In fact, throughout her treatment, I saw God's hand at work. Initially, I was afraid that the medical bills would be financially devastating. Many friends who felt they could do nothing to help wanted to give in some way. So four men got together and set up an account that filled up beyond what we would need. While I was afraid, God had the practical side of things under control.

Take that mundane job I mentioned. I had been working with a customer for several years with only moderate success. However, their business exploded the month Kylie was diagnosed. I worked one week out of the month and had my highest sales number in several years, which made me realize that God can operate my business without me.

I saw God's hand in my relationship with my wife. Although we faced many separations because of treatment, we were always united in what we needed to do. Marriages are often wrecked because of the stress of sickness. We fought together through the whole thing and somehow agreed completely on every terrible decision we were forced to make. I'm thankful for that.

So, you see, God's fingerprints were all over our story. Even at the time, I could see him orchestrating things both big and small, and I assumed it would ultimately be worked together for our good. That expression comes straight from the Scripture I had learned as a boy and taught my children. I believed without a doubt that she would be completely healed and become a living testimony to God's faithfulness and goodness. I remember being on my knees in our basement with her life ebbing away above me, crying and begging God to change direction or take me instead. But that's not the ending he chose. When I asked him to heal her, God said no.

This book is a two-year journey through that wilderness of no. It contains few answers and many questions, but ultimately a faith that there *is* a loving God who chose a path we will never understand on this side of heaven.

From the outset of Kylie's sickness, I began writing about my struggles of heart and faith, mixing humor with heartache and all the while trying to stay as authentic as possible. I have been amazed and humbled by the number of people who reached out to me to say my writing touched them. There are so many people hurting out there, and most don't seem to want to hear memory verses or to have others tell them how to heal as if there is a formulaic bandage waiting to be applied to their wound. They just want someone to hold them while they suffer and assure them that they aren't alone.

I hope and pray some of what you read touches you, too, as you follow me down this twisted path of our struggle, our loss, and the search for meaning in it all. There has to be meaning, doesn't there? Losing a child is so unnatural in our western world – it creates disorder and chaos in a family. We are supposed to bury our parents, not our children. This is hard. It hurts and sometimes it feels as though God has turned his back on me. Yet through it all, I believe that there is a plan God is knitting together through this pain.

I will admit that I don't like God's plan. No matter what comes of it, I would rather have Kylie back. I am just that selfish. I miss that beautiful girl every minute of every day. But, regardless of whether I like it or not, I must abide by His will and find the best way to bring glory to His name while I am still here. Because that's what Kylie would want me to do.

Mark Myers
February 29, 2016

Contents

The Struggle

The Loss

The Search

Epilogue

Appendix

The Struggle

Where Were You?

Where were you when you first heard the sound? Good sounds – your husband's voice, your baby's giggle, the words "I love you?" Do you remember? Can you picture the scene and surroundings?

I experienced a condensed courtship with my wife because I was briefly called back to service during Desert Storm. I don't recall the first expression of the four-letter L word in our relationship. I know it came, and stuck. I have said it to her every day for nearly twenty-two years. I say it every night to my girls and sometimes in front of other people, much to their chagrin.

I wish I remembered the first time I said it, though.

I will never forget the first time I heard the word *cancer* as it related to my family. I was in the hospital just a day ago when it was introduced to me, while my little girl lay sleeping nearby. The doctor actually used the words "oncological event" before I made him dumb it down for me. Cancer.

I held my wife in my arms as she collapsed into a puddle. Doesn't cancer affect other families? Why would he be saying this word? I felt an instant dislike for this man, but my mind clouded to nothing. My wife's head heaved in my chest. I couldn't think in more than three word bursts. I have no idea how long we stood that way. I was roused only by the sound of a man pushing a cart way down at the end of the hall. The wheel squeaked as he carried out his task and I remember thinking, *"How can he be pushing that? Doesn't he know? It doesn't matter where that squeaky cart is! Why isn't he stopping?"*

It was then I realized this isn't everyone's diagnosis. It is Kylie's and ours: our family's, our friends and network of support. But the rest of the world will continue to march on around us.

I will add a link to Kylie's Caring Bridge at the end of this post because I won't allow cancer to dominate my writing. It will peak its evil head in from time to time, I have no doubt. But I won't allow it to take over my life, steal my joy, soil my faith, or crush my little girl.

It took a while to determine the enemy. Until then, we've been punching at shadows. Now we start to take it out. We are at the beginning of a long road, but there is hope. Kylie knows what is going on; she is scared. We cried together and prayed. She has decided that this is happening because God must have a really big, great plan for her. I don't know if I could have gotten to those words so quickly at twelve – she's just chock-full of amazing.

The picture I added is one of Kylie as Annie in her school play a couple of years ago. She is an incredible actress and I can't wait to see her on stage again.

Because our minds are reeling right now, the verse we've been holding onto is Romans 8:26

Likewise the Spirit also helps in our weaknesses. For we do not know what we should pray for as we ought, but the Spirit Himself makes intercession for us with groanings which cannot be uttered. (NKJV)

Thank you for your prayers and words of encouragement, friends. I have to go now, the bell just sounded for round one...

(Caringbridge.org/visit/KylieMyers)

Content Warning

May 6, 2014

*WARNING - This post is not sunshine and rainbows. If you want that, please stop reading now. This is very raw and may be as difficult to read as it was to write. I prayerfully considered whether to post it or not. I know you all want to know what is going on with Kylie and this is the reality of the situation.

In my naive mind, I thought this week would bring us welcome relief from the chemo. I even believed that Kylie might be able to go to school. I suppose that is still possible as it is only Tuesday – but I now see it as doubtful.

I read the multi-page document of side-effects for this poison and somehow still believed that it would begin to purge from her body during this break, giving us longer glimpses of our Kylie. I was wrong.

Some of you have walked this road and know that there are delayed reactions. Once the nausea abated somewhat, the mouth sores started. They have been very uncomfortable. Last night I filled a numbing mouthwash prescription that was supposed to help. It made her nauseous. The acid produced only hurt the sores more – a terrible cycle.

After she calmed from all of that, she cried. I know there was pain in her tears, but I also saw in her face that she wept out frustration, loss, and a lack of understanding about what is going on around her. It was a brutal reality check for me. All I could do is hold her hand. Patrick Moody gave me the sage advice that there will be many situations I can't joke with her through. I'm thankful for that word. It came to mind and I kept my mouth shut and just held her. I prayed for the

Comforter to be with her because I realized that I was completely powerless.

Robin held it together – I have no idea how! As her main caregiver, she has seen this more often than I have. I've thought at times that she was seeing the glass as half-empty and I was the half-full guy. Perspectives can be wrong when you fight the Battle of Bedford Falls and aren't on the front lines 24 -7. I owe her an apology.

Sleep was hard to come by. When Kylie finally drifted off, I had my cry. And I've had a few since. You can ask me if my faith is wavering, and I can honestly give you a resounding NO. I firmly believe we will kick this thing's butt in the end. Scenes like last night's will never be easy, though. I want my energetic, bubbly, happy girl back, but she is hiding inside a weak, tired, chemical-ravaged body. She smiles like the weekend pictures and we know she is there, for that I am glad. We will savor the good times as often as they appear.

Thank you for lifting us up. Obviously, we will need it for the long haul as we are only on mile one of this marathon. At least we are running!

What is That? Fear?

May 9, 2014

We have entered some semblance of a routine around here. It isn't like the old one – that routine is over for awhile. Kylie and her mother being home allowed me to go for a nice six-mile run. The weather is beautiful and it has been way too long since I've been out on the greenway. Of course, that led to some thinking (dangerous for me).

This might sound ridiculous, but we have all avoided public places since the diagnosis. Don't get me wrong, everyone in our lives has been incredibly supportive. We all just find it tough to be in crowds. Her three sisters have had to go to school, so they have dealt with this quicker than I have. I have been working, but I work in a very small office so I don't have to deal with crowds.

Yesterday, our dancer daughter had her ballet recital. My lovely wife and I split up and took in separate performances so one of us could stay with Kylie. While the dancers were beautiful, I found myself very sad when Kylie's class was onstage. I couldn't help thinking that she should be up there, and I couldn't take my eyes off of all of the perfect legs moving across the stage. Hers will be perfect again, it is just going to take time. I came in late and left quickly after it ended to avoid seeing too many people. What is that? Is that fear?

When did I start fearing? I've done some work in some of the worst slums in the world where fear should have been a legitimate reaction, but I felt a supernatural calm. What is this fear? Fear of people who care and show concern... What is that?

I am not an emotionally deep man, but I refuse to live in fear. That's what I told myself as I ran today. Now, I have to decide what I am going to do about it. Am I going to be the leader here, or keep using the three who have faced the crowds at school as shields because I am afraid?

When I am afraid, I will trust in you. In God, whose word I praise, in God I trust; I will not be afraid. What can mortal man do to me?

Psalm 56:3-4 (HCSB)

I'm going to church now. Big step? Not really, but that's what I am going to do. I am going alone because my older girls aren't ready. I totally get that. Maybe I can deflect some of the questions today and next week they will want to go. I don't know if that will work. Psychology isn't my strong suit. But I won't fear.

Battling Armies

May 25, 2014

If you will indulge me, I would like to share about my day. Kylie made us promise that we would go to church instead of coming down to see her. On the way, I called Robin this morning and found out the nutrition doctor had given her the bad news that Kylie's white blood cell counts were not up. That was spiritually devastating to me. Have you ever prayed and prayed for something that you believe has to be aligned in God's will, only to see him say no? That is tough stuff.

I admit I was bankrupt at church, and when Pastor Jon announced the sermon was about spiritual warfare, I thought of five ways to sneak out because it didn't pertain to me and what was going on in my weary heart. I couldn't have been more wronger (As an English major, Robin is cringing at that.)

While this is a medical battle, we are all toe to toe with the enemy for our spirit, our outlook, and our testimony. As I listened to the preaching, I realized that I was fighting discouragement and had yielded valuable ground. When the sermon was over, he had teams down front for anyone who wanted prayer. I have NEVER gone down before, but yielded to the prompting of the Spirit and went with the girls. We were prayed over by a lovely couple, and I felt more prepared to re-enter the battle.

That is where God showed up. What I had no way of knowing while my heart was downcast and I was useless in the fight, was that my God was gaining ground. The original information Robin got was simply inaccurate. Kylie's counts are up. Her white blood cells are fighting the sores and she has requested little pain medicine today.

Some of you may say that this was a coincidence, and I am okay with that. I say that I serve an awesome God who goes before me. When I am weary from the battle, He fights on.

This was a small victory medically. It does mean that if her counts continue to rise, she stands a good chance at coming home tomorrow. After this week, though, this was a huge victory for me spiritually and a lesson I hope I don't soon forget.

I will hand the pulpit back and ask that you pray her white blood cell counts continue to rise.

A Cancer Dad's Psalm 13

Never Before Published

¹How long, O LORD? Will you forget me forever?
How long will you hide your face from me?
²How long must I take counsel in my soul
and have sorrow in my heart all the day?
How long shall my enemy be exalted over me?

³Consider and answer me, O LORD my God;
light up my eyes, lest I sleep the sleep of death,
⁴lest my enemy say, "I have prevailed over him,"
lest my foes rejoice because I am shaken.

⁵But I have trusted in your steadfast love;
my heart shall rejoice in your salvation.
⁶I will sing to the LORD,
because he has dealt bountifully with me.

Psalm 13 (ESV)

How long must my child suffer? How many times must she throw up into a little green sack? How can you stand by, Oh God, while she hurts? The pain is too much, be it the cancer or the effects of the chemo. Don't you see, God? She is hurting!

She cries, oh how much she cries. Your poor child thinks she isn't strong enough to endure. Where are you when she feels weak?

Her dignity is shot to pieces, oh Lord. She has suffered humiliation no child should have to experience. This disease has taken away her hair and stripped her of some very basic self-respect. Her body has done things that would horrify any teen. Yet you withhold. Stand at a distance and watch with the others.

I can't hear her cry anymore! I'm tired of holding her with nothing to say, no way to fix or mend. I am broken. I want to protect her and shout at you with a balled fist in the air. Why?

What will she think if she hears me do that? That I am weak? Doubting? Afraid?

I am weak, I do have doubts, and I am scared... so scared.

She knows that if she stops chemo, the tumor inside of her will grow and she will die. That is the worst conversation I can imagine having with my twelve-year-old. Yet as you have not relented, I had to tell her that very thing. What am I supposed to do when she tells me through tears that she doesn't know if it is worth continuing? She is smart, she knows what that means. Considering what this life has become, is my baby ready to die?

STOP THIS! How long can you wait?

What can possibly be gained from this? If you have monumental plans, can't there be another way? This is too hard.

What are you doing to my poor wife, Lord? She only loves, only trusts, only hopes. Yet now, I have seen her balled up into the fetal position sobbing so hard she can't catch her breath. Please God, don't make me ever see that again. I've held her with no words because I can't promise everything will be all right. Did you hear me when I begged you for something to say – or did her wailing drown me out? What comfort can I give?

How do I lead when I've no clue where to go? Show me the light, Lord. If we are in a tunnel, please give me a glimpse of the light at the other end. The smallest trace will help. Right now, cancer seems like a cavern. I am groping in the dark, bereft of hope.

Will cancer win? Will you let it take away what is most precious? We can't handle that, God. Come now. Stop this.

I am inadequate. Please God, answer me. Show me what I should do lest we fall apart.

Yet even in the midst of this hell, I see you, Oh God. I see your hand everywhere. I feel your presence with me, even when I don't understand. I will maintain that I don't like this – in fact, I hate it. My faith wavers daily until I remember all you have done for me. I am here only because of your watchcare.

I worship you still. You are my only hope – the hope of my child and my wife. Only you can save, only you can heal. I trust not in medicine, but in your provision to those treating. There is no other.

Come quickly, my Redeemer. Free my baby from this nightmare. Defeat this enemy that I cannot. Return her perfect legs to her. Hold her hand as she runs and plays the rest of her days.

I wait for you only.

Baby Steps

June 15, 2014

Many of you will already have seen this on Facebook, but Kylie took her first unaided steps since March today.

We have found that she struggles with fear and gives in all too often. "If I eat, I'm afraid I will throw up – so I won't eat." "When I walk, my ankles hurt – so I won't walk." She took some big steps today, figuratively and literally. I had to negotiate to get her started and she drove a hard bargain. When she conquered her fear and used her walker, she found that it didn't hurt and then she went solo. It was amazing. The pain in her ankles is only tendon pain from being sedentary so long. It has nothing to do with the cancer. There is absolutely no pain in the tumor sites in her knee and pelvis from the exertion, which is most wonderful news. Physically, we have had a great weekend. There is still some pain around the feeding tube site, but it is getting better and is working to get her nutrition. She has more energy and (thus far) has rebounded much quicker from the chemo.

We did hit some rocky waters emotionally. As the father of four daughters, I am used to crying jags and incomprehensible emotions. The beauty of hearing loss is that I can typically tune them out with a flick of a small button on my hearing aids. Seriously, I'm not used to flagrant emotions from Kylie. She is my rock, a wonderfully even-tempered child. As you can expect, the cancer and side effects of chemo have taken their toll on her emotionally. We've all held her numerous times when she has fallen apart. There are no words to comfort, just presence.

Our cat disappeared on Thursday. Not her Stanley, our older Kitty. We have no idea how she got out. She has hidden for long periods before, but after many searches, we figured out Friday that she was gone. This wreaked havoc on Kylie. She cried hard. Robin and I just looked at each other like, "Really? Can't we catch a break?"

After holding her as she fell asleep, I got the flashlight out and searched one last time. My conversation with God wasn't all that saintly, I admit. In the yard, I lit up a pair of eyes. Jenna, Kendall, and I investigated and found it was her, but she was scared to death and ran away from us.

Another day, another big cry and the most pitiful pleading to God from poor Kylie as she cried herself to sleep.

At midnight, Jenna woke me up. The cat was in our yard again. It took some time but our search and rescue party caught her in the playhouse and woke Kylie up to show her Kitty was home. Her relief was palpable. In some ways, I think Kylie was buoyed greatly by seeing a fervent prayer answered. Maybe that's why the cat went missing. Maybe the episode happened just to show Kylie that even when things seem dark, there is hope. I don't know – I'm not bright enough to figure that out. All I know is that today has been a most incredible day.

And that's enough.

And Now We Wait

June 30, 2014

The process went well enough. Coming right out of the hospital, Kylie had trouble swallowing the liquid she needed to. It took a little while to get it down her and by the time we were done, she showed some uncharacteristic anger with Robin and me, but we understand. Funny, once it was over and we were pointed away from the hospital, she was her normal self – laughing and playing in the back seat all the way home. We couldn't be with her for the PET/CT. We talked, prayed and cried a little in the other room. I wish I could say that we had a perfect peace about this. I'd be lying if I did. I have a positive outlook because we have seen progress in the reduction of pain and most of the time, I really feel like God is up to something great here and we will see His healing hand. Most of the time. Other times, there is that voice of despair that whispers the unspeakable in my ear. I have to push it away. One of Robin's favorite verses is:

But this I call to mind and therefore, I have hope.

Lamentations 3:21 (ESV)

Hope is active, not passive... a force of will to change the direction of the mind.

Speaking of my lovely wife, she shared with me what she has been telling God in her prayers for some time during this ordeal. It is simple, yet so poignant that I've laughed about it all day. She has just been telling him:

"She was your idea."

For those who don't know, Kylie is our fourth and was quite a surprise at the time. A stomach ache wouldn't go away. Robin called me at work one day and said, "Pick up some eggs, and oh yeah, grab a pregnancy test, too."

Kylie completes our family perfectly and Robin is exactly right, she was God's idea from the start and he loves her more than we ever could. And so, we wait to see what the next steps are.

If You Can

Never Before Published

I firmly believe Kylie will be fully healed. I feel in my heart that we will travel this road until the tumors are gone, celebrate the victory, and never look back. Maybe it is a childlike innocence. Quite possibly I am not intelligent enough to see reality, or it could be a supernatural peace that transcends my understanding. I don't know, I just believe.

Yet doubt sometimes creeps in.

I believe; Help my unbelief!

The time is early in the horrible process. She can't take her meds to keep her from vomiting. Nausea makes it impossible for her to keep them down and the acid of the vomit washes over the open soars in her stomach and throat causing horrible pain. She cries. We cry. Somehow, she drifts to sleep with mother on one side and father on the other. Neither of us sleep. I sit beside her the entire night watching her chest rise and fall, unsure if it will continue until morning.

I believe; Help my unbelief!

A Sunday starts innocently. In the early afternoon, she complains of a headache that gets worse quickly until we have to leave her in a darkened room. My feeble mind quickly jumps to, "It's in her brain now." I spend hours lamenting that the cancer has spread where it wasn't before. Just before we start the agonizing trip to the hospital, the headache is gone. It was just a headache.

I believe; Help my unbelief!

A cough. A little cough without congestion. Just a tickle. It takes me immediately back to the early stages of diagnosis when they found the tumor in her chest pushing against her lung and causing… a little cough. But the chemo was working. Why is she coughing? Why is the tumor growing again? A day or two and it is gone. It was but a cough, not the symptom of something more sinister.

I believe; Help my unbelief!

And someone from the crowd answered him, "Teacher, I brought my son to you, for he has a spirit that makes him mute. And whenever it seizes him, it throws him down, and he foams and grinds his teeth and becomes rigid. So I asked your disciples to cast it out, and they were not able." And he answered them, "O faithless generation, how long am I to be with you? How long am I to bear with you? Bring him to me." And they brought the boy to him. And when the spirit saw him, immediately it convulsed the boy, and he fell on the ground and rolled about, foaming at the mouth. And Jesus asked his father, "How long has this been happening to him?" And he said, "From childhood. And it has often cast him into fire and into water, to destroy him. But if you can do anything, have compassion on us and help us."

And Jesus said to him, "**If you can!** All things are possible for one who believes." Immediately the father of the child cried out and said, "I believe; help my unbelief!" And when Jesus saw that a crowd came running together, he rebuked the unclean spirit, saying to it, "You mute and deaf spirit, I command you, come out of him and never enter him again." And after crying out and convulsing him terribly, it came out, and the boy was like a corpse, so that most of them said, "He is dead." But Jesus took him by the hand and lifted him up, and he arose.

Mark 9:17-26 (ESV - emphasis mine)

I wonder how much incredulity the Son of God's face revealed when he repeated man's words: "If you can." Silly man. You don't have enough faith. Jesus could easily send the man away and tell him to come back when his faith is enough. He doesn't. The healing of the child doesn't depend on the father's faith, but on the mercy of the Savior.

I have limits. I find my faith is not in endless supply. Jesus, I need you to meet me at the intersection of my desperation, where I have run out and sit teetering on the tracks, just waiting on the impact of the onrushing train. This is all I have. I am dust. I thought I had enough faith. I don't. I need you to fill in the rest.

Help my unbelief.

Will this ever go away? Will I ever have enough? Five years from now if her knee aches, will I fly into a panic, rush to the hospital, and demand a scan to see what is invading her body? Will every bump, bruise, pain, or cough take my weak heart back to that awful day?

Help my unbelief.

Will Jesus always look down on me and say, "If you can…"

Or will my faith grow someday? Will there be a day when I trust her to God fully and rest in his care for her.

I believe; Help my unbelief!

The Strongest Person I Know

August 18, 2014

What is strength? I don't mean muscular strength; I am wondering about the use of the word to describe a mental and emotional strength. Strength of the heart.

The dictionary defines strength as moral power, firmness, or courage.

I've recently seen several quotes about strength. This one stands out:

You never know how strong you are
until being strong is the only option.

-Author unknown

We quote scripture to help us with our strength. Beautiful verses come to mind, such as:

But those who hope in the Lord
will renew their strength.
They will soar on wings like eagles;
they will run and not grow weary,
they will walk and not be faint.

Isaiah 40:31 (NIV)

But he said to me, "My grace is sufficient for you, for my power is made perfect in weakness." Therefore I will boast all the more gladly about my weaknesses, so that Christ's power may rest on me. That is why, for Christ's sake, I delight in weaknesses, in insults, in hardships, in persecutions, in difficulties. For when I am weak, then I am strong.

2 Corinthians 12:9-10 (NIV)

I have been given many more. We read them in times of need and feel their comfort. I don't mean to minimize the impact of the Word – it is all-sufficient. But it isn't always a quick Band-aid overcoming the darkest struggle. Slap this on and feel strong, as it were. I wish it were that simple. In the best of circumstances, most of us need to be reminded time after time before things sink in.

While the concept of strength might be an easy one for you, it has troubled me of late. You see, I am trying to care for my daughter who is fighting cancer. Actually, to be honest, right now she is fighting the chemo that is fighting the cancer. She is only twelve and should never have to deal with any weight so difficult. This road would buckle the knees of some of the world's strongest men, yet she trudges on.

She puts on a brave face and, true to her nickname, smiles to most. But at night, with her mother, her sisters, and me, she often falls apart. The thing I hear from her most often is that she isn't strong enough – she can't do this. I wish there was something I could tell her to change her situation, but I can't. There is no choice, no option, no plan B. The chemo regimen must go on. I wish I could break her cycle of self-doubt, but it is her cycle. I can't change it. I can only encourage and hold, assuring her of my presence and love.

That leads me to my present dilemma: What is strength? Does she have it? If not, where can she find enough to continue when there is no other way?

I think back over her history and wonder if she's had to rely on strength in the past. She has run two 5k races with me and had to reach down deep to finish each one. That took some strength – but not the kind I am looking for. I need her to have strength to say, "This life is worth living and I will fight for it."

My wife has been asking me to add a picture CD onto her computer so she can look at them. After putting it off for too long, I finally complied. The pictures I saw reminded me of simpler times, and I enjoyed scanning them as they flashed across the screen. They were from our school's play, *Anne of Green Gables*, in which Kylie had a part. She barely made it through the performances because of the pain in her leg caused by the cancer soon to be diagnosed.

Wait... what are you showing me, God? Is that strength?

Back up – let me look again.

I see a little girl who was crying herself to sleep every night due to a growing tumor inside her knee. Yet in these pictures she is singing, moving, dancing, and hiding the pain behind a range of her character's emotions so she wouldn't disappoint in the show.

I see a little girl who wouldn't stop dancing until the director forced her to use crutches in the final two performances – and she was mad about that!

I see a girl who collapsed after the finale and couldn't attend the cast party because the pain was simply too great.

Isn't that smiling little girl playing a part on stage the same one who lay in a hospital bed in a medication-induced sleep just a week after the curtain fell?

When told she had cancer inside of her, instead of crying out in anger at God, isn't this the girl who simply said, "God must have a really big, great plan for me"?

Is that precious, animated child the same one who, when she began to lose her hair to chemotherapy, shaved it herself to deny cancer the pleasure?

That is incredible strength! Undeniable strength.

What about now? If we agree that this girl is a strong girl, has four months of treatment changed her? How would a strong person face chemotherapy? Should she charge in, laughing in the face of the toxins that wreck her little body time after time?

Or is it okay to cry, yet move on?

Is strength found, not in the tears leading up to a hospital stay, but in the gritting of her teeth when she allows the nurse to access her port one more time, knowing what will soon flow into her veins?

How much resolve allows a transfusion that scares her to death without saying a word?

What measure of courage is there in quiet submission to a treatment that is nearly as bad as the disease?

An immeasurable amount!

The frail body of my daughter holds enormous strength, and when this treatment is over, I pity the boy who would try to hurt her or the obstacle that would stand in her way.

I have always been big and thought myself strong. I have pushed large objects and run long distances. Yet I realize I am weak in comparison to my frail, eighty-pound daughter, who day after day pushes on through this hell.

She is my hero.

Every morning that she wakes up and greets the day adds to her resolve. There may be tears, angst, cries of terror, and fits of rage – yet every day also contains smiles, kisses, hugs, warmth, joy, praise, and enough laughter and love to beat back at this enemy on her terms.

Oh, she is strong!

My little girl is strength personified, even if she can't see it.

Cdiff & Philosophy at No Extra Charge

August 19, 2014

Kylie started the right antibiotics to treat Cdiff yesterday. Cdiff is common among people in long-term treatment at hospitals, especially among those with weakened immune systems. As I understand it, her bad bacteria has taken over in her stomach. She needs stuff like probiotics, but she can't keep things down. She has been in rough shape. Her fever got over 104 last night, but is around 99.7 last I heard.

While she has felt miserable, she hadn't been in pain until today. That got her this morning, and they reintroduced her to her old friend morphine. I really thought we were through with him.

\<Skip to the end to avoid some philosophical meandering\>

That's the thing. Every time we think one thing is going to happen, the tablecloth gets ripped out by an amateur magician with no regard for our fine china or stemware. This should be her good week between blasts of chemo, and here she is lying in bed hurting. We thought... we expected... we wanted. In the end, "we" have no control. It's hard to give up the reigns – if we ever held them to begin with. I don't mean to be philosophical, but this whole thing creates quite a tension. God has control; we know that, yet it feels as if cancer is calling the shots sometimes. Robin and I are in a little bit of a funk, as you can probably tell. Randomness is a callous enemy.

Many of you have expressed a desire to help, and we are so grateful. So many friends near and far away feel powerless. When we don't know where to put you to work, understand that we are shackled by our own helplessness. And as parents, that is the absolute worst part of this thing – being a spectator to her suffering. And now, climbing down off the ledge...

<Start again here>

Kylie has had antibiotic for 24 hours, and they expect her to start feeling better tomorrow after 48 hours. Please pray for rest and healing.

Camping Out in Hell

August 28, 2014

I've been reading *Hiking Through*, which is a great book about a man who lost his wife, quit his job, and set out to hike the Appalachian Trail. I so want to do that (sans the losing my wife part).

I have always viewed hiking the Appalachian Trail as a journey I probably will never be able to take. But I'd like to. I love hiking and camping but have never been able to partake much since my family hates it. Oh, they like pitching a massive tent in a state park campsite as long as we have sleeping pads, entertainment, and convenient access to the bathrooms. We also can't "rough it" too long – one night, maybe two max. My wife doesn't care for it much at all, but has done it for me and the kids. Maybe someday.

The worst camping I've endured was during my Army days. I was stationed in Ft. Sill, Oklahoma during the summer. I don't think they believe in shade in that state. I'm not sure if there is a religious opposition to it or an aversion to trees, but the sun has free reign there. And reign it does. In the summer it feels like a preview to hell. The kind of place you don't stay in (at least in that season). You just soldier through.

Regardless of whether we are hiking or not, we are all on a journey. We move, we grow, we push on, we persevere. Everyone's journey necessarily involves some hard times – they can't be avoided, unfortunately. In the book, the author talked about being on top of a mountain in Virginia when the roughest storm he had ever seen surprised him. He grabbed onto a tree to wait it out and literally thought he might die. Hopefully, your hard time isn't that bad. But it might be that bad to you.

I can't know the emotional depth of your bad time, and you can't know mine. Every one is unique to the person and situation. I know one thing, the only way to get from Georgia to Maine is to keep walking on.

I stumbled on that Churchill gem recently and love it. I don't know of another quote so small yet so profound.

Keep going.

If I plop down and focus on the misery of my surroundings, they will engulf me in their flames. I have to keep going.

I am hiking through my hell. If you haven't seen one yet, you most likely will. They have a way of sneaking up on you. When it gets hot, I encourage you to pick up your pack and keep going. Camping out in hell does no one any good!

This is an atypically somber post from me. I feel compelled, therefore, to leave you with my own pearl of wisdom:

It is okay to roast a wienie over hell's fire, just make sure you have a long stick.

* *Hiking Through,* Paul Stutzman, Revell, 1992

And God Said No

August 29, 2014

We weren't ready for this. Surprisingly, we got the scan results this morning. While we are glad not to have to wait for them, we are not pleased with the results.

The cancer has become resistant to the current chemo regimen. Here are the facts: The tumor in her lung has grown and is showing activity. It is not to the size it was when we started, but larger than the last scan. Its factory is working once more, and there are new small tumors in her right tibia and fibula. The existing tumor in her left knee has grown slightly. They did not see change in the tumor in her pelvis – it appears to be inactive (our lone piece of good news).

What does this mean? Are we abandoned? Are we without hope? No and No. While we are disappointed and afraid, this simply means we have to change paths. We were already expecting to change paths and begin radiation. Now we will start a different chemo.

Since the chemo they were giving is no longer working, there is no need to subject her body to it anymore. That is a happy thing since Meredith will be home from school this weekend. Before we got the news, Kylie had cried because she had to miss a long weekend at home with her sisters.

She was present for our entire consultation. We made the decision to hide nothing from her from day one. Once she got over the initial shock in April, she bravely asked us never to withhold anything from her and we have not. After the doctor left, we cried together and prayed. Robin said this may be God's way of nudging us to the right chemo. As with the past 22 years, I choose to yield to her as the voice of the Holy Spirit.

Kylie's mood is surprisingly good. The ability to stay at home has rallied her. In previous posts, I've talked about Chemo Kylie and how she shuts down until we get on 400 to go home. This time, she was laughing and joking from the moment we got in the van like we stole the weekend back. She likes the new treatment plan as well. She will get two drugs once a week for approximately 2 months – all on an outpatient basis. These drugs are noted to be less toxic than what she already has taken. So, she hopes to be able to go back to school more during the treatment. She really misses being at school.

Robin and I have had a chance to talk privately. While this is not good news, we agree that this is not devastating. Devastating would be no treatment options. Praise God, we are not there. We both feel deflated and afraid, but not defeated. Deflated because I truly thought we would hear a shocked doctor say the tumors were gone. I had mentally prepared my speech and victory lap and considered the lives that we could impact after God moved His hand on our behalf. I suppose He has chosen another way to reveal His glory. I don't like it, but I trust Him.

As I finish typing this, I am in the den listening to all four of my girls singing together from my bedroom. It makes me very happy. This surprise weekend with everyone at home is a gift. It will be good and we won't let stupid, evil cancer take it away.

Please pray for our new path, for peace, and ultimately for victory and healing.

A Cough

Never Before Published

It wouldn't be a worrisome cough to most parents. It is shallow and dry. It is not persistent or loud. The sound does not rattle. She does not wheeze or choke. The little cough is not productive in the least. In fact, it is hardly noticeable. But we hear it. We try to wish it away and rationalize it, but we know what it means. For us, it means the tumor is back. It means it is growing... competing for space in her chest, displacing the good organ with its evil self.

The cough is our nightmare.

How can I praise God for the cough? I don't want it. I don't want its implications. I don't ever want to hear it again. This plan does not seem wise or loving to me (as insignificant as I am.)

That little cough shakes my faith to the core. If God is good... if he loves my little girl... if he hears the prayers of so many around the world offered up on her behalf... why does she cough?

The chemo was working. We were on the right track – trusting God and coasting down toward perfect healing with the wind at our backs. We laid out flags as markers, set up our stones like the Israelites had done so we could look back and never forget how far God had carried us. We proclaimed his glory along the way.

And now, she coughs.

Now, I cry. I groan. I have no words.

Please, God. Take this cough away. Let her breath free. Work inside this new chemo to destroy the evil inside that wants to kill her.

Silence this cough… For good.

What I Learned About My Wife This Year

October 3, 2014

It is fitting that I spend this day, my 22nd wedding anniversary, with my lovely bride at Children's Healthcare of Atlanta. We are here together waiting for Kylie to get out of minor surgery. We have never made a huge deal of our anniversary – sometimes a nice dinner out, but often there was just too much going on with our four children to make it work. I'm embarrassed to say there have been years when a kiss and a card is all we could muster. Suffice it to say that there will not be a banner celebration this year, either.

Year 22 has been challenging, to say the least. Not in a contentious way, I am happy to report that we have never been more united. But when I review the years, this is one that I would like stricken from the record. I wish I could pull this book off the shelf and let 21 fall lazily into 23. It proves the need for the "better or worse, in sickness and in health" portion of the vows we stood up and said when I was but a wet-nosed pup.

Even though April's cancer diagnosis has made the year regrettable, I have learned much about my wife and our marriage. In fact, I've learned things I will never give back.

I learned my wife has a seemingly infinite supply of tears that no words of mine can dry. My shoulder has been wetted by them far too often. I wish I had a magic word to make them stop, but only time and tenderness sooth the pain.

Likewise, I have learned my wife's care for those she loves has no limit.

I have learned my wife is the most unselfish person I know. She has put her life completely on hold this year and not voiced one word of complaint about what she is missing.

I've shared the boat when the storm is high and seen her reach levels of peace that can only be called supernatural.

I have seen that she can be her loved one's greatest advocate, stopping at nothing to get what her patient needs and letting no one interfere with her.

I know that she might not remember to take her phone off silent for days on end, but she can quickly recall exact medication, doses, and the last time given.

I have found she has strength and resolve I could only imagine prior to this year.

I have seen her ignore her own pain and seek ways to lessen the pain of her patient.

Although she hates camping, I have learned that she will sleep on an uncomfortably hard couch beside a hospital bed for nights on end if someone she loves needs her there.

Speaking of sleep, I have been reminded that she needs very little and will sacrifice it completely if she is needed during the night.

With only twenty-four hours in the day and a relentless schedule of caregiving, she seems to have created time and invented special ways to make the rest of us in the family feel loved.

I now know that her faith, hope, and love are boundless.

All in all, I have seen God reaffirm just how blessed I am that she had a momentary lapse of reason and chose me. I always thought I would be the elderly and infirmed patient that required her care first. I wish that were the case. When I grow old and start falling apart, I'm sure I will test her patience with surprising wimpiness and irrational demands. With what I've seen this year, I know I will be in excellent hands.

So today, I will whisper a Happy Anniversary to her while Kylie sleeps off the anesthesia. Sometimes through sickness and tragedy we learn things. Every day this year, I have seen the tender way she cares for her girl and learned a little more about just how lucky I am.

When I get older losing my hair
Many years from now
Will you still be sending me a valentine
Birthday greetings, bottle of wine?
If I'd been out till quarter to three
Would you lock the door?
Will you still need me, will you still feed me
When I'm sixty-four

-The Beatles
When I'm Sixty-Four

Pure Joy

October 22, 2014

I got to be party to pure, absolute joy this weekend. I have seen such displays on television after a big win in sports or gameshows. This time, it was my little girl who celebrated. After so many losses in the past six months, it was a much needed win.

As a parent, one of the worst things about cancer is being totally helpless. We are forced to sit and watch as one thing after another is taken away from our little girl. Ballet, plays, school, vacations, little things and big things are plucked away as she lays in bed.

Wonderful organizations are out there to give back to these kids. Groups such as the Make-A-Wish Foundation come beside them to give them something to look forward to during their treatment. A very introspective child, Kylie debated long and hard over her wish, finally deciding she wanted to see *Aladdin* on Broadway.

A few weeks ago, Kylie was asked to be the honored child at Make-A-Wish Georgia's annual fund-raising Wish Gala. The chairperson of the event took her on a shopping spree for a gown. This day of shopping was unlike any that my girls have been on – especially Kylie. As a fourth child, hand-me-downs are the rule of thumb. If it isn't obscenely high or dragging the ground, it fits.

Not this time. She was treated like a princess. After a six month hiatus, I saw her old friend, "excitement" start to creep back into her life.

The big night came. We all got dressed up for the Gala.

She knew she was going to sing with her sister. She knew I was going to speak. She thought of herself as the entertainment and the face of wish-children for the evening. What she didn't know was that Make-A-Wish had planned a big surprise for her. They had a video from her favorite Broadway performers who granted her wish to go to see *Aladdin*. Here is her reaction:

Priceless. Pure Joy.

After so many months of seeing her disappointed, I can't look at that expression without tears.

You might be wondering if I embarrassed myself and my family in front of the trendier set. I believe the answer is no. With a stern admonition from the start, I spent the evening minding everything I did and said carefully. I paused three seconds before any word escaped my lips. I didn't spill or break anything. My online tux-buying escapade was made unnecessary by a friend exactly my size who owns a tuxedo. I did not step on anyone's dress or trip on my way to the stage. I didn't try to fit in by discussing the beach chalet I own in Vermont.

It was a lovely evening. Kylie was the star... And she deserves it.

The Wall

November 10, 2014

I don't know how to write this one. It has a happy ending, but sounds bad to start.

Kylie hit a wall. She woke up this morning and was DONE! We have had bad chemo mornings. In fact, it typically starts the night before. So understandable. This one was different. When we discussed starting radiation, Dr. Anderson gave her the choice of whether to start at the beginning of November or do another three rounds of chemo and start in December. To start right away would mean missing a Disney trip we have been offered. It was a no brainer; she wanted to go to Disney and so she immediately decided to suck up three more chemos and start radiation in December.

Last Monday was tough. This morning was impossible. She decided she simply couldn't do it anymore and wanted to call the doctor to see if she could stop chemo and start radiation next week. Robin and I were instantly & totally united. So many decisions have been made without her input over the past year. If she is making a decision, we will honor it.

We warned her that Thanksgiving week would be hard – having radiation while knowing that she could have been on that trip she had looked forward to for so long. Through tears she told us God had given her a peace that this was what she needed to do. Not knowing whether they could fit us in, Robin made the call.

The doctor recognized a kid who was burnt out. He suggested we make today her last chemo and give her next week off. Further, he doesn't want her to miss out on the vacation. So we are staying on the same course of treatment, only she doesn't have chemo next week. Kylie's first response to the news: "God made a way for me not to have all the awful and STILL get the Disney trip."

There are three things I hope Kylie takes away from today.

1. Her parents are in her corner and value her feelings.

2. Her sisters would have been disappointed, but love her enough to give up the trip if it was best for her.

3. God is both good AND great. He orchestrates things for our good even when there seems to be no way.

This has been an emotionally draining morning. I am sitting here in clinic watching her take her last IV chemo. I used to add qualifiers such as, "if this goes as planned," "if the chemo works," or "Lord willing." I decided I need to stop that. In faith, I am sitting here watching her take her last IV chemo. After that, we will enjoy some much needed time off and then endure more separation than I am prepared for while radiation kills the last of this disease.

Pray for her spirit. She has been such a trooper through this whole thing that it is easy to forget she is twelve. For seven months, she's been on a relentless chemo regimen that never let her recover for too long. Enough is enough. I am proud of her for stepping up and putting her foot down.

Cancer for Christmas

December 21, 2014

My wife sat at her laptop furiously compiling the lists for our four girls. She checked it once, then again while travelling to website after website scouring the internet for the best price and delivery. Items were added to baskets and carts checked out at such a frantic pace that I literally felt a warmth emanate from the credit card in my back pocket. Shopping at a fever pitch – Christmas delivered in two days or less. Not like most years, where she disappears for hours on end to find the perfect gift at the mall. She doesn't have time for that this year because we got cancer for Christmas.

We didn't ask for it. It wasn't circled in the Wishbook or written in red crayon. No one sat on Santa's lap and begged for it. No, cancer just showed up unannounced and took our year away.

So rather than spending quality time with each of the girls to weigh their enormous wants against our limited budget as in years past, she spent Saturday morning hunting and pecking under great duress. Do they have the right size? Will it be delivered on time? Is that really something she will use or should we just give her cash?

At some point during the madness, I asked her what *she* wanted for Christmas. She paused to consider. Her eyes got red and her mouth failed her. She didn't answer, but I knew. I knew what she wanted the second I asked the question and Amazon.com can't deliver it, even though we are Prime members. It is the only thing either of us want.

We want our baby to stop hurting.

We want her to stop having to face treatments that make her sick and waste away.

We want her legs to work.

We want her to be able to go to school... to run, skip and play like every normal 12 year-old girl should.

We want her to stop coughing.

We want her hair to grow back so people don't stare at her.

We want normal family time – not garbled, anxiety-laden, jumbled, hodge-podge comings and goings where one is sick or two are missing for yet another appointment.

We want to relax and not worry.

We want to give cancer back.

I'll take one of those please, Santa. Any size will do. No need to wrap it up because if you deliver it, the paper won't last long. Oh, and you can ditch the receipt, I won't be returning that gift.

I know many people are dealing with heartbreak and struggles. While Christmas is a season of love and giving, it also seems to magnify pain and loss. We don't have the market cornered on hurt. I realize that.

It's just that my wife loves Christmas so much. She loves everything about it, from finding the perfect, fattest tree to decorating every square inch of the house in some form of red and green. She loves the sound of the carols (save "Feliz Navidad") and the smell of the baking, even though she is the one wearing an apron. She loves that, for the briefest of moments, the world focuses on the birth of our Savior. She loves taking a drive to see lights on houses and staying home with hot chocolate around a fire. She loves spending time with family, watching *It's a Wonderful Life*, reading the nativity story, and candlelight Christmas Eve services. She loves the mad dash on Christmas morning to see what Santa brought... the joy and wonder on our children's faces. She loves it all.

How do we do it this year?

Should we skip it?

Or should we cherish every moment together as the babe in the manger intended us to? Maybe, instead of focusing on what we've lost, we should hold on to the fragile remains of what we have – love, family, friends, and a newfound respect for the precious thing that is life. We should cling to our little girl, who, though frail, is fighting hard and encouraging others to do the same.

We aren't alone. During the year, we've been welcomed into the country club no one wants to join – the childhood cancer community. While we are bound together by common tragedy, it is the warmest, most caring and wonderfully supportive group imaginable. It is the fraternity I wish I'd never pledged. Many of our new brothers and sisters are dealing with such incredible loss, and this time of year must certainly be crippling.

When referring to the promised coming of the child in the manger, Isaiah said, "...and a little child shall lead them." Isaiah 11:6 (KJV)

What if we took a cue from our little child?

Although she is the one feeling the pain, nausea, and side effects of cancer, she is also the one most excited about Christmas. Even though she only had the strength to stand long enough to put a single ornament on the tree, she admires the finished product and loves to be in the den where she can see it. She is the one who insisted on taking decorations out of town with her while she has to be gone for treatment. She is the one snuggling her elves, dreaming about Christmas morning, and soaking up every minute of the nearness of family and Christ at this time of year. She holds a compress on an aching jaw with one hand and draws up surprises for those most dear with the other. In a year of typically rapid growth for a child her age, she weighs 75% of what she did last Christmas, yet she samples whatever treats her nervous stomach will allow. While we fret over diagnosis and treatment, she savors joy, plucks smiles from pain, and builds a resume of contentment that few on this earth have ever seen. Perhaps she has it right and we have it all wrong.

Instead of looking to health and prosperity for our happiness, what if, just for a moment, we set aside our problems – however overwhelming, and looked to the manger, toward a child – with gratitude for his coming and a longing for his return? What if we laughed in the face of the enemy, knowing that we are wonderfully cared for and uniquely loved? What if we hoped, even when victory was uncertain? What if we dreamed of a better tomorrow regardless of what it may hold?

What if we smiled more?

This joyous Christmas, our family holds on to hope. Together, we look to the manger, to Jesus Christ our Lord for strength and healing. We dream of the day when there is a cure – for our child & every child. We pray that next year, not a single family will have to unwrap cancer for Christmas.

Focus on Positive

December 31, 2014

When life throws you down a crooked track, hold close your family, latch onto new friends, throw up your hands and find something to smile about.

While 2014 was definitely a crooked track for us, I want to close it with a look to the good. Shortly after our diagnosis, I had a friend reach out to me amidst his own health crisis. My advice to him was, *"Hear the negative, focus on the positive and know that God has both covered."*

Good advice? I think so – but much easier said than done. This world screams negative. We are bombarded with the bad. The nightly news covers everything wrong with our world first and longest before they throw in one human interest story just before saying good night.

While sifting through the ruins of this broken world, how do we see what is good? I have seen a lot of things in my 47 years. To borrow the movie title, I've seen the good, the bad, and the ugly. I have driven a man out of the slum of Port-au-Prince, Haiti and watched as he was given the keys to his new home. I have been fortunate enough to help put a roof on a hut in Swaziland for a family decimated by HIV. Beauty plucked from ugly, good snatched from bad. Both started with a choice to engage.

Despite my experiences, never in my life have I seen the good side of humanity more than from the day Kylie was diagnosed with cancer. The flood of well-wishes, prayers, and support for our family has been as overwhelming as the diagnosis itself. When you hear the words, "Your child has cancer," the temptation is to curl up in the fetal position, shut out the world and cry. When I was at my weakest, I found an abundance of arms to hold me.

Friends, family, our school and church rallied to our side.

The nurses, doctors, child life specialists, and staff of the Aflac Cancer Center at Children's Healthcare of Atlanta became dear partners in this journey. We also found great care at Levine Children's Hospital in Charlotte.

Organizations came alongside to help navigate and let us know we aren't alone: 1 Million for Anna, Make-A-Wish, Cure Childhood Cancer, The Truth 365, Rally Foundation, Melodic Caring Project, The Jesse Rees Foundation, Along Comes Hope, 3/32 Foundation, Blessed Beauty, Open Hands Overflowing Hearts, Kingdom Kids, Lily's Run.

We have built a network of people who pray faithfully for Kylie. To be totally honest, I admit there are times when I cannot lift a word to heaven. Maybe a grunt, maybe an angry shake of the fist. Without a doubt, I know there are many people praying for my little girl when I can't. That is incredibly humbling.

Then there is encouragement and love. Kylie gets cards and letters daily. At least a dozen young ladies have donated their hair in Kylie's honor. People all across the country and literally around the world have been #SmileyForKylie. As of today, 87 countries have done it. Grown men have written it on their bald heads.

Between Twitter, Instagram, and Facebook, we have received over 10,000 smiling selfies for Kylie. Unreal. We have gotten them from celebrities, athletes, and Kylie's beloved Broadway performers. Idina Menzel made a video. Kristin Chenoweth made two pics and talked about her on a radio show. Laura Osnes posted a word of encouragement to her. She got a box of Broadway treats from Hunter Foster. She had pics from 9 out of 12 musicals nominated for Tony Awards, and the cast of her favorite show, *Aladdin,* have reached out to her over and over again. Sometimes we can trace the web that led to the picture, but most of the time we have no idea how they happen – we have no line to these people. It's just good. And it is out there – making a choice to engage with our little girl in a time when she so desperately needs it. A thank you will never be enough, but all I can offer.

Regardless of your view of the Bible, Philippians 4:8 gives us sage advice:

> *"Finally, brothers, whatever is true, whatever is honorable, whatever is just, whatever is pure, whatever is lovely, whatever is commendable, if there is any excellence, if there is anything worthy of praise, think about these things."* (ESV)

I'll not be able to change everyone's mind. You can remain a cynic if you choose to. But the things I have experienced in 2014 prove to me that there is good in this world. I choose to think about such things – it is what has kept me going.

In 2015, we look forward to hearing the words: No Evidence of Disease and watching Kylie resume a normal life. That will be something worth throwing up our hands and smiling about.

Happy New Year

Doubt is Like Cancer

January 20, 2015

In a strange turn of events, I decided to listen to a podcast instead of music while I ran this morning. I chose a sermon from one of my favorites, James MacDonald. At about mile 3, I had to stop to replay this a couple of times:

"Doubt is like cancer, it eats away at all that is good."

How relevant, how appropriate, and perfectly timed. It is a fine thing for a day to get a good God-moment in at 5:20 am.

In the spirit of what I took away from that experience, I got text at 2:03 pm from Kylie saying, "I'm cancer free from the neck down!!!"

Yes, my baby has finished with radiation on her lung. Were it not for the thorn in her jaw, she would be home by now. That fact caused a great deal of struggle for both Robin and Kylie on Sunday. It was a tough hurdle for both of them to jump – knowing that we would/should be done today. They did cross it and are pushing through. Once she comes home Friday, she will have a week and a half left. Feb 4th is the end. We knew the radiation would cause some difficulty swallowing, and that reared its head last weekend. All of the side effects are cumulative, and the steroids may have staved it off. She has lost a little weight as a result. The irritation should resolve itself 1-2 weeks post-treatment on the lung. So even though she continues to get treatment on her jaw, her throat and esophagus issues should ease soon. She still is not taking pain medicine often, and the ibuprofen helps very well with the general swelling that was causing her pain before.

This week we were also greeted with the odd news that Dr. Anderson is no longer at Levine. The whole situation is muddled, but Robin talked with him Monday evening and he gave us some advice for the long term. He loves Kylie and is still on our team; we just aren't sure where he will be. Right now, Dr. Crimaldi is the most important member of the team and he is still there. We will finish the radiation, but aren't sure where we will do our scans in two months. The location of that party is TBD.

When I was a kid listening to the Cincinnati Reds on the radio (yes, we did that way back then), Joe Nuxhall used to close every broadcast with, "...*this is the old left-hander rounding third and heading for home.*" That is where we are. Robin and I had a good talk about it on the phone today. If we give in to doubt, we lose the gift of joy we've been given. We have to be confident that this is the end and we are done. Our worry does us no good and certainly does Kylie an injustice. ***"Doubt is like cancer."***

Easier said than done, but we are united in the effort. To keep my Big Red Machine analogy (that Robin would hate, but I'm writing this – not her): If we fear a play at home plate, we miss the thrill of scoring a run.

Please pray for Kylie (and Robin) as they endure another two weeks away from home. Pray for the irritation in Kylie's throat to go away so she can eat comfortably.

And the obvious continual request that this is the end of the road.

The Loss

She's Better Than Me

I've never been much of a poet or poetry reader, but I have always had a favorite poem. It has resonated with me even though I never fully understood its meaning.

Nothing Gold Can Stay
Robert Frost

Nature's first green is gold,
Her hardest hue to hold.
Her early leaf's a flower;
But only so an hour.
Then leaf subsides to leaf.
So Eden sank to grief,
So dawn goes down to day.
Nothing gold can stay.

I understand it now. I understand it and wish I didn't.

I never thought I would be writing this entry. I never wavered in the belief that we would be rejoicing in Kylie's complete healing. That does not appear to be the case. After we left Charlotte, we knew that she had another tumor. We assumed that meant we had more treatment ahead. Things descended rather quickly from there. She started to have pain in two other locations. Very specific, sharp pain that came on suddenly. Even though we tried to tell ourselves it could be something else – the flu or a virus, I think Robin and I knew. The pain was too symptomatic of everything we've experienced to date. We made the decision to go full bore to New York on her Make-A-Wish trip because anything else would devastate Kylie.

But on Sunday, she began to get sick and feel very bad. In the late afternoon, we made that familiar trip to Scottish Rite. Our every intention was to speed healing so that we could have a blast on the trip. We got admitted and spent the night. Kylie was put on oxygen because her breathing became unsteady. In the morning, the conversations I had with doctors ripped my soul to shreds. Terms such as disease burden and incurable by standard treatment were used. I had to make decisions that I am completely incapable of and sign forms no one should ever see. The last 48 hours have been torture. The doctors were all on board with getting her in travelling shape and sending her to New York. Make-A-Wish arranged oxygen there and we were set to go. We decided to let her have this trip before we burdened her with what we were learning.

This morning as I lay on the stupid, red sofa-bed listening to her shallow breathing, I felt a sudden and clear shift. I decided that since we have never withheld information from her, we needed to tell her everything and let her decide. I told Robin and she agreed. And so we had an awful, terrible conversation with our little girl. I watched it sink in. I watched her process it. I cried with her and answered all of the questions that I could. There are so many that are unanswerable. She decided immediately that she wanted to be at home. Home is her balm.

We are not going to New York.

So here we are. What do you do with a little girl who rubs her daddy's beard and tells him it will be all right?

What do you do with a baby who reaches out to console her weeping mother? I watched in awe as she accepted each of her wailing sisters into her arms and one by one stroked their hair and told them everything would be okay. How can the patient be the comforter – especially when she is twelve? It's because she is Gold.

She is better than me.

On a personal note, what do I do with this God? He has provided abundantly for us during this crisis in every way. We have felt loved to an embarrassing proportion. He has bound our hearts together and actually strengthened our marriage. Somehow, we have been united on each and every terrible decision we have had to make. He has given us so many evidences of himself during this time, yet for some reason He has chosen to withhold His hand of healing. I don't understand. What do I do with Him? We have some talking to do, but I have decided that I will follow Kylie in the matter. Somehow, she still holds onto her faith and hasn't given up on Him, so I won't either.

We do not know what the next few days hold. She looks perfect, speaks to us clearly and we all laugh and cry together. But inside, there is an insatiable monster eating away at everything. Our options for further treatment are very limited. We can enter clinical trials, but she has to be 14 days purged of the radiation to even start. We are exploring any option, but her body is so weary it will be a hard call. So we don't know what to do except pull together as a family and love on Kylie.

We aren't ready for an influx of visitors. We will try to respond to texts and emails as we can and will read comments and try to share them with Kylie. Soaking up every minute with Kylie is our main focus. Thank you all for praying for us and encouraging her with your smileys. We aren't giving up and continue to pray for a miracle.

Love Remains

February 12, 2015

I have searched for a way to describe yesterday. It was awful, terrible, and yet somehow beautiful. It was packed with struggles, heartache, love, and memories of better times. Kylie slept a good bit of the time aided by medicine to keep her pain down. Local family descended upon our house where we talked, cried, and prayed.

When she was awake, Kylie was very alert and enjoyed spending time with us, Super Smash Brothers, home videos, and *American Idol* Hollywood Week. Like the past year, Robin has barely left her side and that's the way they both want it.

It is the understatement of the year to say this is hard.

We have home Hospice now. They have been wonderful at helping us make sure our baby doesn't hurt anymore. That's what is important. We have made some difficult decisions that we could only make with the information we had at the time. But they have been quickly confirmed. I have always felt like she received excellent treatment, but I have a newfound respect for our doctors and the staff at CHOA. They worked so hard to honor our desire to take Kylie to New York, even when they knew we were fighting long odds. I saw their write-up in the Hospice file. The cancer has progressed at a staggering rate over the past week – much further than we suspected. I won't detail it because it is immaterial. Suffice it to say, the beast is everywhere. The docs knew that and still did everything they could to help us go. I will thank them soon.

Kylie hasn't been awake very much today after she got her baby kitty and she was barely awake for that. Somehow, that curious, rambunctious little kitten hasn't left Kylie's arms, even though she wouldn't lift a finger to stop her. Kylie has been on oxygen since we got home. Her breathing is labored, but she is comfortable.

I find myself extremely angry that right now she should be taking the stage at the New Amsterdam Theatre for a curtain call with the cast of *Aladdin*, yet she is lying in bed struggling to breath. Soon she will be introduced on a different stage to a much more glorious audience. While I am not ready, she is perfectly cast. Her costume and makeup won't include baldness, a g-tube, or a port, and her dances will be flawless on perfect legs.

She has given Robin, me, and her sisters our charges. We family have orders that we will see to. While smiles will be hard to come by for a time, love remains. We are forever #SmileyForKylie.

Kylie passed away the following evening. February 13th, 2015

God is on His Throne

February 18, 2015
My eulogy for Kylie

Besides marveling at my keen fashion sense, you might think it foolish for me to come to the podium. But I've never been one to heed good advice or shy away from making a fool of myself. I am here because I have a point to make, and I need you to hear it and I need you to remember it. It is what Kylie would want you to know.

God is on his throne.

This wonderful school has taught my children that repetition is helpful to learning, so I want to repeat my point, just in case I have to exit the stage in tears.

God is on his throne.

Many of you know that Kylie was a huge surprise. Thirteen years ago, Robin had a persistent stomach bug. One particularly tough Friday, she called my office and asked me to get a pregnancy test on the way home just to rule that out. Remember that we already had three daughters under 6 years old at the time! So along with the test, I picked up a gallon of ice cream just in case.

In the morning, she woke me up holding the ice cream, a spoon, and the positive test and said, "Eat up, big boy."

Our life has never been the same. The name Kylie is Australian for Boomerang, so named because the girls kept on coming.

We joke that we stole some other family's first child because Kylie had all the typical tendencies of an eldest child. She was a perfectionist, eager to please, and a diligent worker. She was always our sunshine.

Joyful. Loving. Our peacemaker. She gave the best hugs. From her earliest days, we called her Smiley Kylie because a smile was never far from her face.

I learned a lot about Kylie over the last year. I saw more of her tears than a father should ever see. I saw her bite her lip while a nurse pumped poison into her body, knowing that it would soon make her retch.

I always thought I knew what strength was.

I didn't.

At a frail 75 pounds, Kylie was the strongest person I will ever know. During her treatment, there were tears, angst, cries of terror, and fits of rage – yet every day also contained smiles, hugs, warmth, joy, praise, and enough laughter and love to beat back at the enemy on her terms.

Kylie will forever be my hero.

I don't understand why this was God's plan for Kylie. I have struggled with that every hour of every day since we knew her death was imminent. The question is, does it matter if I know?

I also don't understand quantum physics, gravity, women, the rules of punctuation as they apply to semi-colons, and most basic mathematics. Yet they still exist. If I never learn any of them, that doesn't make them less real or binding.

So it is with God. While I may never understand his plan, that doesn't change the fact that he is on his throne, He is good, and He loves us. During the past year, He showed himself real to us over and over again, yet for some reason, he chose not to heal. Why? I do not understand.

Being Kylie's social media coordinator, I got a unique glimpse into people's interaction with our little girl. I had to filter and delete some things, but I want to read to you just a few of the messages we got over the year:

Early on, a man began reposting nearly everything we put up. I thought it odd at first, but then saw that he wrote this:

This girl is awesome! She has changed my heart on many things.

That little statement was my first glimpse into this special thing God was up to with Smiley for Kylie. It only got better. One woman said:

I have been praying for you to feel well enough to go to your Gala. Honestly, I have not prayed for anything or anyone so fervently in over a decade. Thanks Kylie for bringing faith back to my life. Your daily strength gives me a reason to have faith in God again.

Another:

I just wanted you to know that our family prays for Kylie and through her journey and faith, she has brought us closer to Christ. Because Kylie's story weighs on our hearts, we find ourselves praying more not only for Kylie, but more often than we did in the past. Kylie, through your struggles and faith, you have changed our spiritual life. Thank you.

Listen to this young lady:

I began following your Facebook page as a student in nursing school and realized that God has called me to focus my work on childhood cancer. Before every test, I would make a list of names of people who inspired and motivated me to keep studying and do my absolute best. On February 6th, I received my nursing license with Kylie's name on the top of my list.

Here is a favorite of mine:

I have been so selfish in my past and am guilty of the poor, pitiful me garbage. However, since I began to follow Kylie's page, I have changed as a person. You are so positive and strong. Seeing your posts reminds me every day that no matter how bad I think something is in my life, there is always hope. I do not know you personally, but you hold a place in my heart and soul. I pray for you every day and I want you to know that every day you are an influence on my thoughts and the way I perceive things that happen. It's kind of a "What would Kylie do?" situation… and most of the time I think to myself that Kylie would smile and just dance.

Even this week, they came:

I love her because she always had a smile that would brighten your day. I never smiled. I didn't know how, until I saw Kylie's post. She taught me to live! I had given up on life and all in it. Thank you for sharing her with us.

Wow! That's my little girl! And it is just a small sample. I wish I could honestly say that I have affected as many people in my 47 years as she did in her 12.

So what would Kylie do with this God that we don't understand? To answer that, I'd like to read you something from Kylie herself.

We've made so many new friends along this crooked path. We met other patients who encouraged Kylie and sought encouragement. One of these is a beautiful young lady in Illinois who suffers from a chronic illness. She reached out to Kylie over some fears of an upcoming scan. Listen to Kylie's response:

I know what scanxiety is like and can understand what you're feeling right now. Recently, I had the scan that revealed the tumor in my jaw. It was scary going into that scan because of the immense amount of pain in my jaw, but a previous scan had made them think it was not a tumor, so I wasn't expecting the news. I'm praying so hard! Scanxiety is the worst. Don't ask why, but look at what you know, and admire what God has shown you. I think it is easy to focus on what could happen. Instead focus on what wonderful things have happened and that God has a plan for what is ahead.

Kylie impacted the lives of so many people, but why did she have to lose hers to do so? I don't know and I may never know. But I know that God is on his throne, and because Kylie told me to, I won't focus on unanswered questions. Instead, I will focus on the wonderful things that have happened... like the 12 years she graced my life. I encourage you to do the same.

Maybe you were the kid who finished their test before everyone else. Maybe you were like me and had a page full of holes and eraser shavings, scrambling through question 7 when the teacher called time. Many of the teachers here can attest that Kylie was an excellent student who finished her tests on time. We've talked in the family and want to assure you that Kylie didn't die early. Her life was perfectly complete.

She finished the test. She got an A+. It only took her 12 years where it will take most of the rest of us much longer.

Over the past year, I've taken so many pictures with this phone, many that you will never see because Kylie always had full right of refusal and often said no. Kylie would be shocked and humbled that so many people are here today. If you'll indulge me, I'd like to take one more Smiley for Kylie of all of you in your yellow. And you have to smile whether you want to or not – because that's what Kylie would do.

"If there ever comes a day when we can't be together keep me in your heart, I'll stay there forever"

-Winnie the Pooh

To see a video of this eulogy, please visit:

http://bit.ly/KylieEulogy

Missing Kylie

February 22, 2015

I have been absent from posting for a few weeks. The reason is that Kylie took a sudden turn for the worse and left her battered body on February 13th. I miss her every day.

There are so many questions and very few answers. My lovely wife and I had to plan out her funeral, which was truly heartbreaking. During the discussion, I felt compelled to speak at the memorial because I knew that Kylie would never want anyone to waver in their faith because of her passing. So I did. It was one of the hardest things I have ever done, but I made it through.

There is no formula to recovering from this type of thing, but I think we are doing as well as can be expected. We intend to grieve well and then get on with the two charges our little girl gave us – Mommy has to take care of her kitten and I got the easy one: cure childhood cancer. Her social media sites are exploding so she is handing us a platform for it, which we intend to use. Right now, we have no idea how… But we will figure it out because Kylie told us to.

The Search

A Very Special Letter

Never Before Published

During her treatment, Kylie began corresponding with an adult friend who was in the midst of breast cancer treatment. They developed a beautiful relationship. We never read their letters, but received this surprise in the mail soon after Kylie died. It is a precious gift and the last letter she wrote.

Dear Mrs. E,

I want you to know that these notes mean a lot. It's comforting to have someone who <u>actually</u> understands <u>personally</u>. So many people say they do, but there is so much more than the brave face people try to hide behind. But somehow I think the truth I'm learning is worth it. Not many learn it, thankfully. Everyone wants to, but they don't want the journey to it. I don't want them or I to go through it. But you never know how much you need God's strength until your strength is not enough. And the beauty and light in the worst of it, is the prettiest and most blinding. Even a sunrise brightens my day. I imagine God's paint brush, and I wish I could dream up the colors on his pallet.

I've seen beauty in things that don't seem beautiful. Like when I knew I <u>couldn't</u> do chemo anymore even if it meant losing the Disney trip so we called the doctor and he said if I did one more instead of two I could go anyway. The pain leading up to not being able to handle it was hard, but the wonderful words of the doctor were one small glimpse of the overall beauty of God's plan. It showed me how much he cared.

Even my feeding tube is both terrible and great because it makes it so I'm not forced to eat.

I made a chain of how close I am to the end. It is getting short, and it brings me great joy when I look at it. I'll be honest, video games make me happy! I'm a kid after all!

I completely understand loving your son being home. My sister went to college and she comes home every weekend. I really miss her when she's gone. And treatment being in Charlotte is killing me. Not being able to go home is the worst, but I'll do it to kill cancer, or as Bailey and I say Evil Dr. Tumor! We wrote a comic where we are super heroes and he is the villain! And I'm so excited about Tom Sawyer! I can't wait!

Sorry about the essay! I got carried away. Thank you for the letters. God bless you. I love you!

> Your friend,
>
> Kylie

P.S. I will be on my Make-A-Wish trip on February 15th. I wish I could go to your party, but hopefully by then we'll both be celebrating no cancer! I will be cheering for you from New York!

Also, my radiation machine looks like a duck, so I named him Quakers.

A Cat's Divine Appointment

Feb 25, 2015

Did you ever believe in a divine appointment? I mean, something that worked together so perfectly that it had to be orchestrated by God in order to unfold properly. Something that, if man touched, would fall apart like a house of cards built on a rickety three-legged table.

It happened to me recently. Actually, it happened to a cat I now own. If you've been to my house or been reading my blog for any length of time, you know our pet burden is already far too high. All rescues, we have Winston, the huge, stupid, lovable lab. Toby Flenderson, the dog with a personality deficit. Kitty, a barn cat who came to live with us two years ago. Stanley the Chemo Cat, a sweet, fat boy who was chosen by Kylie to sit with her during treatment.

In the last weeks, our little patient wanted a baby kitty. Actually, she has wanted one for some time, and I was able to say no. At one point, I bought a bottle, put Stanley in a diaper and tried to pass him off for a kitten. He was pretty cute, but a 14 lb. cat doesn't pose well as a baby.

So, when we got the terrible news that her disease had progressed, I could no longer say no to *anything* she wanted. I called a friend who knew a pet rescue organization and in a few hours, a kind lady from Angels Among Us delivered a baby kitty who had gotten off to a rough start in life. We had every intention of returning the cat in a few days.

This is where the divine appointment came in. We brought the kitten to Kylie who sat up for the very last time to welcome her. She gave us her last smiles and loved on that little cat as long as her energy would allow. When she laid back to rest, that little kitten curled up in the crook of her arm and never moved. Never! If one of us moved her, she walked right back into the crook of Kylie's arm and laid back down. Eliza didn't move from that spot until Kylie breathed her last.

You might think we got a mellow, lazy kitten. You would be wrong. She is rambunctious, curious, and now runs and jumps all over the house. She is an amazing leaper who rules the roost. She won't even take crap from Winston, who feels a perpetual need to sniff her backside until he gets a claw on the nose.

The mere fact that she laid so still for a day lets me know that she had a job to do – a divine appointment. She did it perfectly and now we will spend the rest of her life rewarding Eliza for her job performance. She is our baby now even though the last thing we need is another pet.

We all believe Winston is too stupid to realize this is a new cat because he hasn't seen all three of them in the same room together. He probably just thinks one shrunk.

I wonder if we all have divine appointments at some time in our lives, but don't sit still long enough to realize they are happening.

How Are We Now?

March 13, 2015

Another Friday the 13th. Is it truly possible that it has been a month? It seems so long ago sometimes and sometimes it seems like yesterday. Then there are brief interludes of fantasy when I dream it never happened and life is normal. My rational brain won't allow those glorious moments to last nearly long enough.

The last Friday the 13th – the bad one. I carried her. I had carried her frail body so often over the past ten months, it seemed natural. Only this time, she didn't wrap her arms around my neck or tell me where to go. This time, our destination wasn't the couch or the kitchen table. On that dark evening, I carried her to the hearse waiting in my driveway. I did it because I didn't want anyone to see her loaded onto a stretcher inside my house. How could we ever recover from that sight?

It was the longest walk I've ever made.

The visitation and funeral are a blur. Pictures and video tell me they happened. I remember seeing so many friends. There were times I was almost happy except for the specter of grief that always pulled me back into its dark bosom. We spent another ten days with very little activity and a great many tissues. The void created by the passing of a relatively small child is disproportionately large.

So how are we doing?

I asked Robin that very question and was given what I thought was an incredibly simple yet insightful answer.

"Everything feels wrong, all the time."

Wrong. Off. Askew. Like staying together in a hotel where a home used to be. *Wrong* like when I had to drive my truck after it had been broken into a few years ago. *Wrong. Stolen from. Unsettled.*

Yes, we have played games, shared laughs, and had fun, but everything always settles back into this *amissness.* The tears come and go. None of us try to force an end to them, we just huddle and wait them out. Nothing specific triggers them – just a Kylie-sized hole.

Sleep is a game that Robin and I play differently. She can't find it; I can't keep it. So she stays up and reads or hangs out with our night-owl teens until she gets exhausted. I fall out at my usual time. But when my eyes open at 3 or 4 am, I am awake for the day. As time has moved on, the rules of the game have relaxed for both of us. She gets to bed sooner and I rise later. Still not normal, but better.

We have thought about getting away for a weekend, just the two of us. Maybe it would be good to reconnect. Funny thing is, we've been connected throughout this horrible experience. We've been on the same page the entire time and are hesitant to give up a moment with the girls. Jenna is nearing the end of her freshman year, and from experience we know that the rest of high school will fly by. Kendall will be a senior next year – we will be empty-nesters soon enough. Then she will have nothing but my mug to look at, and my guess is that she will feel way too connected with me. I know, it's only a weekend, but we've learned just how precious a few hours can be.

If I haven't said it enough, my wife is incredible. She gets out of bed every day and pours love over the four of us. Taking care of her girls is what gets her up and she is laser-focused. After a year of being somewhat on their own, they are over-loved, over-conversed, and over-mothered right now. They might not admit it, but I think they are enjoying it. Robin gets out of the house a little now – not a ton, but more. She doesn't like long trips or long visits. Short is good; short doesn't require a lot of preparation or conversation.

For me, I have loved seeing pictures and videos of Kylie from before cancer came to stay. I don't want to forget the past year; we had some great times of joy amidst the suffering. I would, however, like to minimize the final couple of days. I feel the shift happening, but not nearly fast enough. As a father, my principle job is to protect. While my head knows cancer was out of my control, my paternal instinct at times whispers accusations.

I still lack focus. Things seem to happen around me, and sometimes I can almost detach from a conversation and watch myself participating in life like an eerie third party. It is so weird. A year ago, I prided myself in being able to keep a dozen balls in the air without dropping any. My first few days back to work I dropped everything like an amateur juggler. I might be up to four now.

So, how are we?

It's still a pretty dumb question. We are parents living in the aftermath of the loss of their daughter. We are about as good as you'd expect. We miss her every minute.

Still, we have hope and faith that we will see her again.

We have each other, and we have you friends who have read this far.

If you want an honest answer, we aren't doing well, but we are better than we were a week ago and certainly better than the last Friday, the 13th.

I am not sure how, but I think we're going to make it.

Why I Turned Right

March 25, 2015

This was not the ideal day to run a marathon, nor was I in shape to run one. A constant rain fell on us from the time we started, leaving me the choice to pull a race-day decision of shortening the run by half. No one would blame me.

When I had signed up, we thought Kylie's treatment was going well. Running the marathon to raise money for pediatric cancer research seemed to be a great thing to do for other children who would follow us. Her decline came so quickly. One of the most minor consequences of her passing was that I no longer cared about training. When the date came close, although not ready, I decided to run – well, walk and run. I knew it would be a long day. Of my two running-mates, only Krish was prepared. Randy's knee had prevented his training.

We talked beforehand and I espoused my belief that there would be no shame in turning left at mile six and completing the half-marathon. No shame at all. It seemed the logical choice.

We lost Krish in the crowd early on, and we wounded two ambled toward the split, not knowing what the rest of the day would hold. After running four miles, my back began to ache. It wasn't debilitating, but we still had twenty-two miles of pavement to pound… or possibly a wiser nine.

When we got close to the split, I wanted to go left. Already hurting and unprepared, the thought of the full scared me. Decision time had come.

"What do you want to do?" I asked.

"I kinda want to finish the drill," Randy replied. "Just think of the accomplishment!"

I didn't want to do it. I thought he was probably crazy enough to finish it alone. My back cried out that it was a bad choice. I hurt. I ached and I was about to move left and send him on his way when I thought of Kylie.

So many times during chemo, Kylie hurt. So many times, she ached and cried out that it was too hard – she couldn't do it. She wanted to stop every day, but she kept on going. She persevered even though she didn't know when it would stop. When she was throwing up from chemo, she couldn't count down from twenty-six to one, knowing the nausea would subside with the numbers. It just went on and on for her. I knew the exact end. There was a palpable finish line waiting for me. The end of the misery called "treatment" for cancer never came for her. She died before her treatments ended.

The thought of her triggered emotions for me, mixing tears with the rain on my face. I knew there was only one choice. I turned right. I turned right for Kylie. How could I not finish this race when she pushed so bravely through hers?

We trudged on for twenty more miles. It wasn't pretty. The rain never stopped and the pain persisted to the end. We walked a good bit, but ran at the finish as if we'd been running the entire time. It was finally over.

I bent to receive a medal that I wish I could put around her neck, but I can't. I can't because we don't have safe and adequate treatment for childhood cancer, which is the very reason I ran in the first place. The medal will always be hers, though. And someday, I'll tell her about it and how I thought of her and turned right.

The End of Why

April 5, 2015

She came to me as I woke this morning. We greeted many days together while the others slept, my morning flower and me. Kylie was my only early riser and a sweet little sunrise companion. She often invades my thoughts in that twilight of sleep when the mind isn't quite sure if it is still at rest or engaged for the day – could reality be that the sickness was the dream and she is soon to beg me for a sip of coffee while we whisper to let the rest sleep?

No, it isn't the case. I felt her clearly this Easter morn as I lay in a strange bed. Through the generosity of friends, we escaped the routine of the holiday where the egg hunts, chocolate bunnies, baskets, and church in frilly dresses leave too big a hole. Too hard. So, here I sit on a porch overlooking a quiet lake as the sun rises over the water. My coffee is mine, although I'd give anything for her to mooch it. "Why's" as endless as the waves lapping the shore are my only company.

Why did you give her just to take her away?

Why would you let her suffer? **Why** not take her quietly in the night instead?

Why couldn't we have had one more week to enjoy the trip she yearned for?

Why? Why? Why?

Why is a bottomless hole.

I am sure the disciples fell into that hole. As they scattered throughout the city afraid for their lives, it had to be their preeminent question. I wonder what their **why**'s were. I can guess. **Why** didn't you fight? **Why** did you lead us on? **Why** did I leave my family and career for this? **Why?**

I have learned that God is not often inclined to answer the question **why**.

One day, when I get to heaven, I can't wait to ask him. It's the very first thing I'll do…

But wait. Hold on. The **why** is in the way!

When I get to see Jesus face to face, it will be because of the very atoning sacrifice that we celebrate today. I will see him only because of the death and resurrection that drove those questioning disciples into hiding. When I see him, there will be a little girl with long brown hair and a perfect body holding his hand waiting to introduce me to him. In her other hand she might hold the most sumptuous cup of coffee that she's been excited to share with me.

Why won't matter.

Why will have died.

Why is but a temporary distraction.

Why stayed in the tomb.

Whatever your questions today, praise God that through his Son, **why** only matters a little while.

The Frailty of Fair

We've talked a great deal about the concept of fair of late. An odd word, fair. If you look it up in the dictionary, you will find it has nearly seven times as many definitions as it has letters. The one that pertains to our conversation is:

Conforming with the established rules.

Children all over the world cry daily, "That's not fair!" I have a daughter who has a justice meter and feels that everything should line up equally. If things do not, she will protest the unfairness of the situation. She gets that from my lovely wife, whose righteous indignation will rise at anything wrongfully appropriated. Things must be fair.

But they aren't, are they?

Fair is a myth. Oh, we try. We make rules and establish laws to make things as fair as humanly possible. But there is something bigger at play. There is an overarching fairness that we can't comprehend. When we put things in their cosmic proportion, we can make things as equitable as we want to and they will never be fair – because we are not in control.

Tell the orderly little ant about fairness when he is marching in the line, doing his job, and he watches fifteen of his co-laborers get stepped on by the careless human. Sometimes, I feel like that ant. I've seen the footfall of God land on someone I love. His concept of fair is different than mine.

It isn't fair that Kylie got cancer. No one can explain how it happened. They told us that somewhere along the line a gene mutated, and boom, a tumor appeared. Random. It isn't fair that she started doing so well only to fall victim to the silent spread of the disease. Likewise unfair is that she had ten torturous months of treatment.

While she was in treatment, she met a housekeeper in the hospital whom she loved. Ms. Nikki made her smile. Whenever Nikki came in to do her job, she made it a point to talk to Kylie, encourage her, and always seemed to find a way to make her laugh. She was sunshine on many awful cloudy days. Early on, Nikki and I started doing a "Going Home" dance together on discharge days. I assure you, she was a much better dancer than me and Kylie always wanted to find her before we left so she wouldn't have to endure my solo.

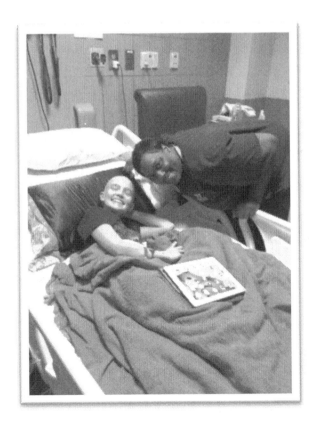

On a trip with her children recently, Nikki's car was struck by two cars going in excess of one hundred miles an hour. Two of her children were ejected from the car and killed on the scene. The third died at the hospital a few days later. In an instant, the wonderful Ms. Nikki lost the three things most precious to her because of someone else's carelessness. Where is fair?

Death is never fair – be it instantly or after a long illness. It leaves too much pain and too many jagged edges.

My heart cries out for Nikki – for her loss, her pain. While I am grieving my own loss, I cannot imagine hers. I pray for a peace that seems as unattainable as fairness in this broken place.

I wish I could make things fair. I never will be able to; neither will you. The only thing we can do is love those we are tied to as long as we are here and as long as they are here with us.

Snuggle Mommy

May 10, 2015

Rob Petrie had it made.

He had the love and adoration of the beautiful Laura. He had a fine young son. He had a fulfilling job where he worked in a humorous family atmosphere and neighbors who were his closest friends. You know what else he had? A good night's sleep! He got a good night's sleep because he and Laura had separate beds. Can you imagine it? I can. You see, I'm not one for snuggling.

I blame the fact that I get too hot. But really, I just like to be on my own. I think I've always been that way. I don't recall a time when I just felt an overwhelming urge to cuddle. Oh sure, we were honeymooners at one point, way back in the early 90's… when I was young. I am sure I snuggled then. But like any guy, if I were honest I would admit to an ulterior motive.

All of my daughters are snugglers, and when they were young, somewhere between one and four of them would appear in our king-sized bed during the night. When we had daughter 1, Mommy would bring her in to get some sleep after a late night feeding. Who was I to stop them? I was of no use at feeding time. Besides, I was comfortably asleep on my side of the bed. My desire to be separate was used against me because I didn't notice the intrusion.

Daughter number 2 had a doll bed on wheels that stayed beside her. Whenever she woke up, she would push the loaded bed down the hall. Even the canopy was laden with dolls because evidently dolls are like soldiers – *no doll gets left behind*. Daughter number 3 didn't have a bedroom until she was a year old, so she started the night in a cradle at the foot of our bed and always seemed to join our merry band.

And number 4, well Kylie was the chief of all snugglers. As the baby, she never lacked someone to snuggle. I even snuggled her sometimes because she just fit.

When she got sick, we all snuggled her any chance we got – no one more than mommy. As her caretaker, mommy snuggled her in the hospital and at home. They read together, knitted together, watched television together, and just sat together – most of the time arm in arm. The one time Kylie preferred someone other than mommy was when she wanted to play video games, because mommy stinks at those. We all encouraged gaming to steal an opportunity.

Pretty much the only way to get kicked out of bed with Kylie was to sniff her bald head. Although it smelled like heaven on earth, it ticked her off for someone to smell it.

I miss those snuggles.

After she died, a friend with the same unfortunate experience told me I would hear her voice someday. It didn't take long. I heard it soon after the funeral and it was as clear as a bell.

"Snuggle Mommy," she told me.

"Huh?" I tried to argue, "I don't like to snuggle! I miss you. Forget about snuggling, let's talk awhile."

She had but one message. I could almost picture pursed lips and a cocked head as she repeated it slowly so it would sink into my thick skull, "Snuggle Mommy!"

I wanted more, but she was gone. Her image and voice faded away.

I knew she was right, though. Mommy needs snuggling. Since Kylie died, mommy had taken to snuggling Buttercup, Kylie's big chemo bunny. Ten months of a constant companion leaves many unexpected voids. Mommy needs snuggling.

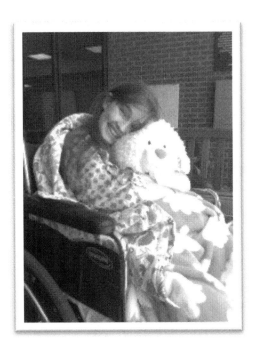

And so, in the past two months I have snuggled like I've never snuggled before. I'm trying. While I miss my aloneness, I have noticed that when you bunch together, the covers don't get pulled off as much. It is weird not being on my side of the bed, but life is weird right now anyway so what's a little more weirdness? Also strange is snuggling without that old ulterior motive.

Okay, I admit there will always be a glimmer of hope… I'm still a guy, after all. But hey, it isn't the main reason.

What Jesus Didn't Do

May 17, 2015

Yesterday we attended a dedication of some benches at the local high school. Our freshman daughter wanted to support a friend whose brother died last year. I'm proud of her for asking to be woken up on a Saturday. I am equally proud of about a hundred kids who got up early to celebrate with this boy's family. They even put their phones in their pockets for twenty minutes! It was heartwarming.

There are times when you think you are doing something for someone else and God has different plans. I thought I was going out of respect, but I was deeply moved by the event. We can uniquely and unfortunately sympathize with parents who have lost a child. While we have so many questions about Kylie's death, as the parents of a child who took his own life, they have more. None will ever be answered, but we can navigate storms together.

A young man named Darren, who is a student pastor at North Point Church, opened and briefly discussed John 11:35. Brief is the right word for it. The shortest verse in the Bible and a favorite of young boys everywhere who are forced to memorize scripture.

Jesus Wept

(I would add a translation note, but I think it is all of them. In fact, this might be the only one that scholars agree on.)

People most often try to theorize why Jesus wept. Was it because he loved Lazarus? Did he weep for the mourning sisters? Or did he cry because Lazarus was experiencing the perfection of heaven and he was about to pull him back? There is no knowing the answer and I am frankly tired of unanswerable questions.

Darren didn't make an attempt at an explanation. What he touched on wasn't why he wept; he talked about what Jesus didn't do. Brilliant! WWJD has become an iconic acronym, yet here we have an example of **WJDD**.

Even though he is the God of comfort, he did NOT give it.

Jesus Wept

Although he is the all-knowing God, he did NOT give an explanation of why it happened.

Jesus Wept

In that instant, he did NOT tell them what was going to happen.

Jesus Wept

He did NOT provide answers, even though he was the only one privy to them.

Jesus Wept

He participated in their sorrow and just cried. Before his God nature took over, Jesus allowed his human self to grieve with the sisters. Beautiful Tears.

Let that be a lesson to us. The next time someone in your life is going through heartache, loss, or sorrow, remember that words will almost always fail, and there will be time for action later. Take a cue from what Jesus didn't do, and simply weep with them.

The King and His Walls

June 3, 2015

There once lived a king of a small but beautiful castle. He had everything a king could want – a beautiful queen, lovely princesses, bountiful land, friends and plentiful resources. He was also quite proud of his walls. He had built them sufficiently high and strong so they could withstand attack but not so foreboding that they repelled callers of good repute.

Near his castle were other industrious kings, all working toward the common good of the people and the land. These small kingdoms lived in relative peace, save the occasional border dispute – always quickly solved with diplomacy and understanding. To the north lay a massive kingdom that ruled the entire known world. It was long-rumored that this land was perfect and its people well-loved. Inside that castle was a good and great king who treated the lesser kings with abundant mercy. Although this king had the power to easily crush any rival beneath his feet, he preferred to rule with honor, civility, and justice. The smaller kings attempted to emulate this king in every facet. Always generous in his teaching, the good king sent letters and even a royal emissary to instruct in his ways. And the people were better for it.

One day our king noticed an unfamiliar soldier staring up at his walls. He called, but the dark soldier ran and hid in the surrounding forest. With little cause for alarm, the king went about his duties until he saw the strange soldier again – this time very close to the wall, inspecting it for weakness. The king yelled down once more, and once more, the soldier fled.

Days went by and the king fell back into his work. One night, however, a harbinger came and told him his walls were under attack. With no time to spare, the king ran to the wall and looked down to see an army of dark soldiers preparing for war below.

"Wake the troops; send for our allies," he called. "We will defend our walls!"

Messages sent to his fellow kings far and wide were answered immediately. From the moment of the siege, allies rallied to the cause. Some were intimate friends, some merely acquaintances, and many were men our king had never met. Of course, the great king to the north sent every resource requested. Even in this dark time, because of the support, our king felt a warmth of love he had never experienced. He marshalled his troops, beat back at the enemy, and for a time seemed to be repelling the attack.

But the darkest days of the war came. Rocks and stones tumbled from the wall, each one hurting our king in ways he didn't expect. Though his friends never wavered, he knew more was required.

A messenger was dispatched to the great king of the north requesting men and weapons. To our king's dismay, the messenger returned with a large supply of riches – gold, diamonds, and rubies. Knowing these were of no use to him in his current dilemma, the king once again sent his messenger. This time, he made certain the message was clear – men and weapons of war were required.

To this request, the great king sent eloquent letters of love and encouragement.

Frustrated, angry, and confused, our king once more wrote a desperate message in his own hand begging the great king for what he needed.

The messenger returned empty-handed.

"He gave you nothing?" the king shouted above the sound of his castle's demise.

"When he read your letter," replied the weary messenger. "The great king only wept and said, 'tell your king that I am with him.'"

This saddened our king, for he knew all was lost. The barbarians were quickly upon the defenders. In a final push, the wall came down. The loss was great. Although the defenseless kingdom was now theirs for the taking, the invaders seemed content to leave the king exposed and melted back into the forest.

But what of our king?

Our king stood atop his ruble looking out over tumbled walls, carnage, smoking debris, and immeasurable loss – broken. All that he had presumed to own was no longer his. The safety of his walls proved to be an illusion. Never before had our confident king found himself at a loss for direction. But now he fell into utter confusion.

Should he rebuild these walls or find a different way to protect his kingdom? Although he had built, he did not know how to rebuild, and from where he stood, there seemed a vast difference between the two. How would he build the walls high enough to protect... to stop the pain... to quench his aching heart? And what of the great loss?

How would he ever reconcile the seeming indifference of the great king?

One by one, old friend and new marched past our lonely king and offered condolences and aid for which he was grateful.

Yet when they were gone, he stood alone among the ruins.

And for the first time in his life, he had no idea how to lead.

Artwork: Henry Dawson - *Nottingham Castle: King Charles I Raising his Standard*

Coming Home

Never Before Published
A fictional response to the tragic deaths noted previously in The Frailty of Fair.

"Hi! I've been waiting for you," the girl said warmly as she hugged both of the new arrivals.

The newcomers felt a tad overwhelmed with their surroundings. They had no fear whatsoever; there was just too much to take in. So many beautiful sights and colors danced before their eyes – more than they had ever seen in their lives.

"You have a lot of people ready to see you, but I asked if I could show you around first," she explained. "You see, I knew your mamma."

"Is she here?" asked the youngest child with her beaded hair bouncing as she scanned right and left for a sign of her mother.

"Not yet. But she will be."

"When?"

"Oh, it won't seem like long. It's the strangest thing, time doesn't feel the same here."

"What does that mean?"

"Well, you know how you had to wait for things there, and sometimes it seemed like what you were waiting for would never happen?"

"Like school to end?" asked the older as the memory struck him.

"I was thinking more like Christmas to come," laughed their guide. "But yes, I suppose that's true, too. It never feels like you are waiting here. Sometimes things take a little while, but there are always good and fun things to make the time go by."

"What kind of things?"

"Whatever you like!"

"I like playing ball," he replied.

"Here," the girl said as she bent to pick up a brand new baseball the two children hadn't seen before.

The boy took it in his hands. He squeezed the leather and ran his fingers slowly over the bright red seams.

"We better not take this," he said, offering it back to the girl. "It doesn't belong to us. Somebody will miss it and get mad at us."

"It's yours," said the girl. "I promise. No one gets mad here."

"Really?" asked the youngest. "What about when you do something wrong."

"You don't do anything wrong."

"Ever?"

"Nope. Never."

A twinkle fell across the little girl's eyes. "Lucky our big brother isn't here, he does wrong things all the time... then blames us."

Their guide laughed. "He's coming soon. Remember how I said time moves differently here?"

The children nodded.

"Well, it's been three days there already, and he will be here any minute."

"Whoa," said the littlest. "Really?"

"Yup. You like to paint don't you?"

The girl betrayed a look of confusion. "Yes, but how did you know?"

"It's very strange, but you just know things here. Look at this pallet," she said as she led them toward a small easel standing beside a large oak tree. "Have you ever seen so many colors? This one is my favorite. I call it Frintiple."

"It's like yellow, but brighter," exclaimed the girl in awe. "I love it! Oh, but I like this one best."

She pointed to a color somewhere in the pink family that showed an unbelievable iridescence.

"We could stop to paint awhile," suggested the guide. "I love to look over that valley and paint it, especially at sunset. It's the most beautiful thing I have ever seen. I'm not very good, but I'm getting better. I've met some famous artists here, and they give me lessons sometimes."

While she continued, the boy wandered over to a fully set garden table.

"Would you like to eat?" asked the guide.

"I think we were on our way to dinner before we came here… Yes, we were going to McDonalds" the boy recalled. "But for some reason, I'm not hungry anymore."

"You never get hungry here, but you eat whatever you please. And it is way better than McDonalds!"

"Better than their cheeseburgers?" the little girl asked indignantly while her hands slid to her hips. "Nothing is better than those!"

"I promise," smiled the guide. "Why, I have a chocolate fountain in my house that I dip everything in. It's wonderful."

"Oh, you better be careful," warned the boy. "Mamma said you'll get fat if you eat too much chocolate. She only let us have one piece a day."

"Would you believe me if I said you don't get fat here? And you don't eat too much, either."

The two children looked at each other with wide eyes of wonderment. While the tale seemed too fantastic, both of them instantly believed.

"I feel like we should get back to where we met you for some reason," the little girl said.

"See, you're getting it now!" affirmed the guide. "You just know things and have these feelings, and they are right so you do them. We should be getting back there because Jaylen is almost here."

"How did you know…" the boy started to ask, but stopped and smiled. He knew the answer before he finished the question.

The guide held out her hands. "Would you like to skip with me? I like to skip because my legs didn't work so well before. You see, I had cancer and was in the hospital a lot. That's how I met your mamma."

"I'm a good skipper," said the little girl as she and her brother joyfully took their guide's hands and turned to go.

"Do your legs work now?" asked the boy.

"Perfectly. Just try to keep up," she answered with a sly little grin. The three of them sauntered away together, racing but not competing – just enjoying every second.

"My name is Kylie. After we get your brother, you have a lot of people to meet. Lauren, you look just like your grandmamma. She's a wonderful lady who helps me with my knitting. And Jorden, you'll love your great-great granddaddy. He was in the Army and tells the best stories…"

They beamed at the thought of meeting family they didn't know existed.

"Will you do something with me?" Kylie asked as they arrived at the spot.

The two children smiled in reply.

"Your mamma and my daddy used to do a silly dance every time I got released from the hospital. We called it the *Going Home* dance. I thought maybe we could dance for Jaylen – kind of a *Welcome Home* dance for him. What do you think?"

With radiant light in their eyes, the two children giggled and began shaking themselves to a rhythm only they heard. Their guide joined in as they laughed and danced to welcome the next arrival, who appeared in his perfect time.

Don't Read This Post

June 17, 2015

Disclaimer: Don't read this post if you prefer only happy thoughts today. There are plenty of other posts better suited for that on this blog and others.

This post is sad.

This post is heartbreaking and uncomfortable.

This post relays some of the realities of burying a child. It hurt to write and will likely be hard to read.

Once you read this post you will know – and you can't unknow what you know.

If you want to stick your head in the sand and pretend that we are doing enough to cure childhood cancer, this isn't the post for you.

You've been aggressively and sufficiently warned. You might want to stop reading now. I won't think any less of you, I promise. I admit that I turned my head away up until a few years ago – but now I know, and I will forever know.

Two things happened on a Tuesday last month – one planned and one a surprise.

We had a piece of unfortunate business to attend to. Many of you have been through the death of a loved one and were responsible for the pragmatics of laying them to rest. This was our first time. We had been putting it off, but if we wanted a grave marker for Kylie, it had to be designed.

So on that Tuesday, we went to the funeral home where Kylie was buried. Nothing about being there was easy. Even though it is owned by dear friends and I've been there for countless funerals, it screams of the day we buried Kylie. I remember planning the service, the line of people at visitation, saying goodbye to her, holding my crying girls, and the sinking feeling of permanence. Worst of all was the shock of sitting in the back of a car when the casket came out carried by my seven nephews. I don't know why that moment was so poignant. Maybe it was the sheer surprise of the door opening or because I wasn't doing anything. I had no role at all. Like during her treatment, I was relegated to being a spectator. Whatever it was, those young men emerging with that box will forever be etched in my mind.

This time, we sat around a table and talked. Earlier I had asked Robin to think about what she wanted on the marker. She had never mentioned it and didn't show up with notes. But when asked, she rattled off what she wanted and it was perfect:

Kylie Elise Myers
Loved with abandon
Radiated joy
Changed us all
Feb. 24th, 2002 – Feb. 13th, 2015

Soon after we finished that piece of business came the surprise. It came in the form of eight copies in a manila envelope. Eight copies. Eight copies that reaffirm what I know every day. Eight copies that make me feel helpless, weak, and insufficient. Eight copies that bring me to tears as I read entries such as MARRIED: NEVER...

Never means never.

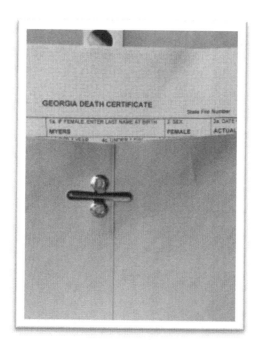

I hadn't thought about getting these documents. I suppose I need them. I'm not sure what for – she didn't have a trust fund to dispense or a will to execute. She was just Kylie, 12-year-old Kylie, and now she is gone. I feel her gone-ness every minute of every day.

This is how it is when you lose a child. The thing we had to do was difficult, but sometimes easy things like accepting an envelope devolve into an emotional crisis and break you into a puddle of tears.

We had driven separately and I cried the entire way home. I think seeing the death certificate brought back feelings of failure as a father... that I didn't do enough to protect her. It felt so real and concrete, carved in stone.

I managed to keep the envelope away from Robin's sight and stowed it into the safe with our other family records. Birth certificates, passports, insurance policies, marriage licenses, and now our first death certificate. Oddly, according to the state of Georgia she died of respiratory failure, not the insatiable beast of cancer. Maybe that is how the government rationalizes the fact that since 1980, only three new drugs have been approved specifically for use in the treatment of childhood cancer.

Wait! What? Did you hear that?

While hundreds of drugs have been approved for adults in the same time span, children are dying and getting next to nothing. In this age of genetic discovery, children are receiving a pittance... table scraps.

And so, Kylie is gone. I have eight copies of her death certificate to prove it, and unless we step up and do something, other parents will get the same envelope.

I feel about as helpless to affect government spending as I did watching her body capitulate to cancer.

But you read this. And now you know. You may choose to ignore, but you can't unknow. Maybe that's a step. And if you tell someone, then they will know, too.

Breakfast in Bed

June 21, 2015

For as long as I can remember, Father's Day started with breakfast in bed. Actually, since I wake long before my brood, it started with me milling around, then getting back under the covers to feign sleep so they could "surprise" me with breakfast.

I would never have told them, but I hated breakfast in bed. I liked the idea of it but not the practice. All four of my girls would bound into my bedroom with excitement, hand over a brown tray filled with biscuits, jelly and coffee, then leave me to have their own breakfast in the kitchen. Off in the distance I could hear them chatting and giggling as they ate with mommy. On the very day meant to celebrate my role in the family, I sat alone wiping jelly on the sheets because whichever one was napkin-bearer neglected her duty. Strange custom.

They have passed the age where breakfast in bed is fun. In fact, as teenagers they now believe that mornings are a punishment sent from old people to rob them of their joy.

I don't miss breakfast in bed. But there is something missing.

People have always had odd reactions when they discover I have four daughters. Some make jokes, some say they are sorry, and some just stand open-mouthed, trying to put themselves in my shoes. It's okay, I've heard them all. I don't remember a time when I took offense to anything anyone said, because it doesn't bother me. I love my girls and believe I was given exactly what I was intended to have.

I once came up with a clever response like, "With so many kids, if one turns up missing, we will never know."

Only it's not true. It was a stupid line.

I miss the little one like crazy and I always will. The chair at the table will always be hers. The room at the top of the stairs, sink in the bathroom, seat in the van – all hers… forever. She has left little time bombs all over our lives that detonate randomly – a computer file named *KyliesDoNotTouch*, her signature on a basement wall stud, her bald Mii character on the Wii game system. The bombs bring both laughter and tears when they explode.

And yet, I wonder. I wonder if I am often focused too much on what was taken and not what remains. The great loss makes it hard to appreciate fully the uber-talented actress, the creative genius, and the graceful dancer who all at one point flopped onto my bed as curly-headed breakfast servers. They are amazing young ladies. So, while I will forever be proud to be called Kylie's daddy, I am equally proud to be called Meredith's daddy, Kendall's daddy, and Jenna's daddy. I hope they know that. I will tell them today.

If I have learned nothing else over the past year, I now know that life comes with no guarantee. The next breath you take may be your last. Likewise, the same holds true for each and every person you love. If I hold enough sway to offer any of you advice: tell them now. Love them now. Don't wait a moment because the next may not exist.

The hole in our family will never be filled, and it seems especially deep on days like today. While much remains, there is and forever will be something missing.

You know what else is missing? An end to this post because I think I hear them rumbling around with the tray in the kitchen. Oh crap, I gotta pretend to be asleep!

Our Greatest Fear

July 22, 2015

What is your greatest fear? What is it for you – that thing that gives you shudders just to think of it? Thunderstorms? Dogs, snakes, spiders? Heights or maybe confined places? Perhaps it is something psychological like public speaking, failure, or being alone. Most of us are afraid of death. Everyone has something they fear in varying degrees – even Chuck Norris.

Your list of fears might be long or it might be short.

While I don't love snakes, I know my greatest fear is being eaten by a shark. What are the odds, right? I go to the beach one week out of the year and stay in the surf. Oh, I wade out and play. But I always I keep a wary eye on the horizon and make sure there is at least one person bobbing between me and the deep blue. I call him chum and he is my harbinger. When the shark pack pulls him under, I figure I'll have enough warning to swim to safety.

As a child of the seventies, I blame Jaws. Sharks didn't exist for me before then. I am not sure if I had yet visited a beach when I saw the movie. In my young mind, the Florida coast became full of twenty-five foot man-eaters that could beach themselves for the right meal. A boy doesn't just get over that. Yes, sharks are my biggest fear.

At least, they used to be my greatest fear.

As grieving parents, my wife and I are now living out the greatest fear of many – the fear of losing a child. Except when at the beach, I am an eternal optimist. I never in my wildest dreams thought this would happen to us. This sort of thing happens to other people, and we are the type who rally to support them. Even when Kylie was diagnosed with cancer and the prognosis hovered at 30%, I didn't waver in my belief that we would win. I wish I could take my chances with a shark instead because I can avoid saltwater and remove any possibility of attack. Unfortunately, we fell on the wrong side of the percentage, and the resulting grief is much like a shark. It is cold, unpredictable, and unrelenting at times. It uses triggers, but doesn't require them. It sets traps, lies in wait, and springs at inopportune and random times. Losing a child is something to be feared.

At one point, we sat down and listed the things we lost when Kylie died. We lost joy, sweetness, hugs, and our peacemaker. We lost patience, enthusiasm, and energy. Our artist is gone. A lovely soprano and incredible actress has left the stage. We no longer have an affiliation with our beloved school – it was stripped from us early. We lost potential… seemingly unlimited potential. We lost a great deal – yet I find I don't fear most types of loss much anymore.

In fact, I don't think I fear much of anything. I still have a healthy respect for the killers of the deep, but even death has a strange allure because my baby will be waiting there.

You know what I do fear?

I fear you'll forget her.

I fear that her image will get fuzzy and fade away.

And that is what I believe is the greatest fear of anyone who has lost a child: that he or she will be forgotten. We fear that because their lives were cut short, they won't matter enough for anyone to remember. Our children didn't live to accomplish what they were supposed to accomplish – the things that would make them memorable. So, how will the world ever mark their short time here on earth?

That is why so many foundations and charities are created in children's names. It is why songs, poems, and books are written in their honor. In the great search for the meaning of a life cut short, we parents yearn for another soul to share our mission to remember.

Do you remember Kylie? Do you have another friend who has lost a child? I can't speak for them, but I love hearing stories about her – things I didn't know before. Not only does it tell me that she was special to that person, it lets me know that someone else is helping to keep her flame from being extinguished... that I'm not alone in this awful vacuum. I just want to know that even though she left her potential unfulfilled, her life mattered.

Here is my point and my charge. If you know a bereaved parent, tell them you remember. It doesn't have to be much. Just something that will let them know they aren't the lone bearer of the candle.

Someone saw a play recently and went out of their way to tell me, "Kylie would have loved that!" I later saw a friend of hers who told me how Kylie had made up a pretend brother in the second grade. Both were small gestures, yet meant the world to me. They know... They remember... she's with them, too. Her life had meaning to more than just me because her memory remains clear to someone else.

Our fears may not be the same, but we all fear something. You can quite possibly allay another's greatest fear today by assuring them their child will not be forgotten. It may not seem like much, but it may keep them above water for one more day.

And we all should stay above the tide because I know what is lurking down below...

The Empty Chair

August 5, 2015

We have spent the last week at the beach – a familiar condo we've visited several times. When the summer schedule was being formed, there was no question whether we would go. At issue was how hard it would be without Kylie. She is an ever-present mist coating our lives, so almost everything is hard. But not everything holds an opportunity of mingling the hard with fun. This place offers that.

In fact, I'm sitting here now typing this in a room of bright yellow. I never noticed the vibrant color of the common room before. Yellow has a new meaning for me these days. It is early morning and any previous summer she would soon walk out of her room rubbing her eyes and push my laptop aside to sit with me. She would ask me what I was writing, and I would usually tell her a Virgil Creech story while she mooched my coffee. Sometimes if she was still tired, she would ditch me to go snuggle her sleeping mommy. But most of the time, I got some precious alone time with her. I had no way of knowing just how precious it was.

Shortly before she died, Kylie told her mother and me that sitting at the edge of the water digging her toes in the sand with a book was her favorite place. We all love that. In fact, I just finished my third book since we arrived. Every morning we carry chairs down to the beach and spend a majority of our time reading. It is spectacularly hard not to dwell on the sadness of the empty chair.

We chose her gravesite based on that. As we were being driven around the cemetery in a stupor, we came beside a small pond, and we both told the driver to stop. He informed us that this area was more expensive, a fact that normally would cause me to reconsider. In this case, it didn't matter. We chose as close to the water as we could get so our baby could dip her toes in the water forever.

Everything is hard. Everything is sad.

So here we are at the beach and Kylie screams out at us constantly. It has been as advertised: both hard and fun.

We've laughed at the memory of Kylie's stubbornness. As a fourth child, she felt the pressing need to keep up with her sisters and always insisted on carrying her load. The chair she preferred has backpack straps, and the first few years here, that chair would rise over her head and nearly touch the ground. Undaunted, she made the trip every day.

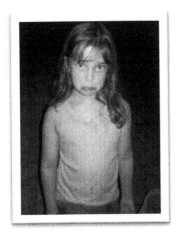

One year we discovered crab hunting. Kylie named our first one Cinderella. We were about to name the second when we made another discovery… crabs don't like sharing space. So we named number two Mike Tyson and had a cage match. We sat ringside until Kylie's big heart could stand the fight no more, and she made me release them.

Never one to be left behind, toddler Kylie put on water wings and came as far out in the surf as we did – even when we talked of sharks. We affectionately dubbed her "chum" and wrote a song we would sing as we encouraged her to bob further out in the water. She loved that.

Other memories pour out of us, and sometimes tears. It has been nearly six months. There is no expiration date to sadness. Grief will always have its tentacles close enough to latch onto us. But I find on this trip, for this moment in time, my memories have been mostly happy ones of a girl we love and miss.

I am not naïve enough to think myself magically healed and restored. I never will be. I am broken forever. The heart is said to be an involuntary muscle, yet this year I have had to force mine to beat at times and imagine my life will be spent jumpstarting it when it is clogged with sorrow… until that day when it will no longer turn over.

At the beginning of the week, I received a text from a friend who simply said, "I hope you are feeling close to her there."

I love reverse logic and am just dull-witted enough to suspect that it has been used against me all of my life. I like the way my friend chose her words. Instead of focusing on the hard – the **Distance** and separation, she hoped for us to feel **Close** to her. Take negative and substitute positive.

This question ferments in my mind: Is it a choice to feel **Close** or to feel **Distance**? Like I force my heart to beat, can I force the same heart to feel close to her instead of missing her terribly? I typically feel so distant from her that I could circle the moon three times and not catch up. Am I choosing that?

Or maybe there is a cosmic tug-of-war and **Distance** is simply stronger than **Close**. The big, muscle-bound jerk **Distance** spits, glares, taunts, and pulls me to his side more often than not.

I don't know which it is, but I'm certain that greater minds than mine have studied the matter. In the end, I do not believe that I always have a choice in how my broken heart feels. While I can have some sway over them, feelings are feelings and often rage beyond my control. Grief and **Distance** make a formidable team, and I fear I am only the little flag in the middle of the rope helplessly watching *Close* get yanked into the mud pit time after time.

On the drive down, I dreaded missing her more. But in reality, I have felt closer to her here as I'm surrounded by people she loved in a place she loved. I'm glad of that. Maybe our little friend, *Close* has been working out.

The Snake I Didn't See

August 12, 2015

Did you know that a snake can lunge and envenom a person for up to an hour after it has been killed? Seriously! What power of darkness is this?

I learned that fact when my children were very young. We live in the woods and have taught them the rules about snakes: see snake, run screaming from snake. One day they were bounding down the steps to their cousin's swing set when my eldest saw one on the path. She stopped the merry procession and called for me.

It was a bad one. A fat copperhead stubbornly coiled on a short retaining wall at a child's eye level. In fact, one of them had passed within a foot of its mouth before they spotted it. There was no angle to use a shovel, so I had to resort to my brother-in-law's rifle. I am an excellent shot, but don't own a weapon (Unless you are a criminal or young man with bad intent interested in one of my daughters, then I have an arsenal).

Locked, loaded, snake shot nearly in two. Problem solved, right? One would think. I proceeded to use the shovel to move it to the driveway. It was slithering a little, but I didn't think about it. After all, its head was nearly disconnected from its body. About halfway up the stairs, that broken snake made a desperate lunge for my leg. Luckily, I saw it and dropped the shovel with the snake's fangs about a half an inch from my calf. I left the minion of evil slithering around itself on the steps for a few hours and made the kids play inside until it could be properly disposed of.

The whole thing gave new meaning to the phrase: *if it were a snake, it would have jumped up and bitten you.*

There was another snake this week. Its camouflage was perfect and it came out of nowhere to bite me. I can see most relevant dates on the calendar and predict their emotional impact in this season of grief – any holiday, her birthday, the anniversary of diagnosis and certainly the date of her death will be forever marked with a big red X on the calendar. The first day of school lay hidden in the weeds and bit me hard Monday.

Eight years ago, we took Kylie to first grade. Mommy had to wear sunglasses so the others wouldn't see her tears. It seemed that Kylie's classmates were all first children, while she was the youngest of four. Some of the kids cried and held onto their mommy's legs. In our case, quite the opposite was true. The younger parents must have thought us an old couple who had pleaded for a child (ala Abraham & Sarah) as we unpacked her, said goodbye, and sat on a bench outside the classroom while mommy wept. Leaving her there meant being at home alone, and mommy likes having her little eaglets in the nest.

Last year, Kylie bravely fought to be at school. She was sick and exhausted from chemo but determined to be there. Mommy sat nearby that day as well, in case she needed to go home early.

Last Monday should have been her last "first day" at our beloved Perimeter Christian School. She should be the big kid there – an 8th grader. We should have gone back-to-school shopping in the previous weeks, and if treatment had gone as planned, she should have had hair. She should have been able to walk the halls on her own. We should have taken pictures of the reunion with her classmates and hugs with teachers.

We should have had more. Kylie deserved more.

The first day of school pictures Monday were just like that snake lunging at me – only this snake connected. I don't begrudge anyone posting them. The pictures are part of the routine – the parents and children deserve that routine despite the effect it might have on me. It is just hard to see normal. Cancer stole normal.

And yet... I love those kids and that place. Once I dropped the shovel, I found a great deal of pleasure in seeing how much they'd grown and remembering how well they loved my little girl. Kylie's friends are

142

starting to look like little adults, and their beautiful smiles slowly won the day.

I know there are bad snakes lying in wait, but I have learned that there are good snakes also. While some don't agree, one year I killed two large non-venomous snakes, and the next year my problems with the bad ones doubled. You see, good snakes eat bad snakes. The only surefire way to shed myself of my snake problem is to never go into the woods.

Here's the rub: I love walking in the woods. There are so many good things in the woods that I won't allow the occasional bad snake to ruin the pleasure of a hike among the trees. It may just take time and a couple of good snakes to nudge me back on the path.

I Never Dreamed

September 2, 2015

I used to be a vivid dreamer. I don't know what a psychoanalyst would say about this, but I had a constant companion in my nighttime capers – a penguin named Pingy. He wore his hat backwards and always had on sunglasses hiding bloodshot eyes. He was a bad seed, that Pingy. One of those affable, fun-loving friends who always seems to get you into trouble. Half of my dream life was spent rescuing him… often from the law. It has been a long time since he has visited me. Life has a way of clouding out frivolous dreams with its deadlines and demands.

When I was a boy, I dreamed of being a third baseman for the Cincinnati Reds. Somehow, Johnny Bench, Tony Perez, Joe Morgan and Dave Concepcion, although in their forties, would still be All-Stars and welcome this rookie into the fold. Together we would form a dynamic team – The Big Red Machine, Part II. Fame, riches, women… they would all be mine. At that age, I likely had no idea what the women were for, but I understood better as I got older.

For the record, a vivid dreamer who is also a sleep-talker can be a dangerous combination for a newlywed. Yes, we are still married despite this.

In all my dreams, I never dreamed it would be like this.

For so long, I had it good – The American Dream. A good job, nice house, two cars, lovely wife, and an endless stream of kids we couldn't seem to figure out how to stop. We've never been rich by U.S. standards. However, I've had the privilege to serve outside the country in some poverty-stricken nations, and there I found that middle class in the U.S. is a king's life in most places.

Maybe you're like me. Your life seems to speed up every day with the bustling of family. Schedules and to-do lists become endless tomes that prevent sleep. And when you finally enter that deep REM sleep where a friend like Pingy peeks into your frazzled mind, a curly-headed ragamuffin jostles your arm and whispers, "Daddy, there's a monster under my bed."

Even through the hectic weeks, you often realize that you *are* living a dream – and it's a good one. That although the major leagues never came calling, things have been set up pretty nicely and bonus – you don't have to deal with any pesky rotator cuff pain. You understand that you have more love and beauty in your life than any man deserves. Four little sets of eyes look up in awe and reverence and call you daddy. They color pictures of you with a stick body and oversized googly eyes. For a time, they even wait excitedly for you to come home and mob you when you finally arrive.

It is a good dream. But just like any, you have to wake up.

But I never dreamed it would be like this.

I never dreamed tears would become a part of my everyday life – whether I see them, wipe them, cry them myself, or stifle them.

I never dreamed I would see my little girl in such pain, hear the word cancer, and watch her carted away for surgery after surgery.

I never dreamed I would be so helpless.

I never dreamed my beautiful daughter would be bald.

I never dreamed that childhood cancer is sometimes incurable. I assumed sick kids got better.

I never dreamed I would plead and bargain with God only to receive a resounding "No" as I knelt beside the bed of my sick daughter on her last day on earth.

I never dreamed she would die, even when I heard the odds and knew it was likely. I never dreamed...

I never dreamed I'd be such a loser – because this is losing. I lost regardless of whether I had any ability to affect the outcome.

I never dreamed I would walk down a corridor and receive so many looks of sympathy.

I never dreamed sleep would be so hard to come by... that I would become afraid to dream because dreams are either fading images of the former good or nightmares of the current emptiness.

I never dreamed one of my children would be relegated to photographs and memories.

I never dreamed life was this fragile.

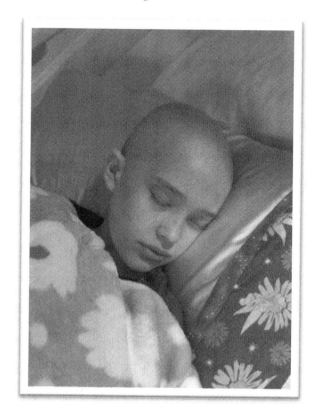

September is **Childhood Cancer Awareness Month**. Cancer is a rabid thief. It steals many dreams. It stole Kylie's dreams of performing on Broadway, painting a masterpiece, driving a car, falling in love, and having her own family. It stole our dream of watching her blossom. While vast sums are spent by the United States Government and the American Cancer Society on cancer research, very little goes toward childhood cancer. There is a common misconception that adult drug therapies will trickle down and work for children. Unfortunately, that is rarely the case. In the past twenty years only three drugs have been approved by the FDA specifically to fight childhood cancer. This has to change. We need safer and more effective treatment for our children, and that will only happen if we join together and demand it.

My dream is now for your children.

Free Awkward Hugs

September 23, 2015

I have never been comfortable with the manly hug. I can't tell you why – I think man-hugging is one of those things you either experienced as a youngster or didn't. I didn't. I'm more of a firm handshake kind of a guy. That's my zone. I learned early to give a girl's father a firm squeeze and look him straight in the eye as you say hello. I appreciate my dad teaching me this skill because it makes a great introduction before you load yourself, your date, and your dubious intent into a beat-up jalopy to go out for the evening. Eddie Haskell had nothing on my teenage self, Mrs. Cleaver. The good news now is that an old Eddie can spot a young Eddie immediately. They've come to my door hoping to see my daughters. The minute that kid takes my hand, I look into his gleaming eye and send him packing. Of course, he just lowers his head and leaves because he knows he got busted… it might take a minute, but a young Eddie can recognize an old Eddie.

Current circumstances have taught me much, and I am certainly learning the comradery, affection and compassion wrapped up in an embrace. I have another cancer dad who tells me I'm getting better at it.

I think I may have hit my stride this weekend.

My family came to Washington DC to honor Kylie's wishes to spread awareness of the need to find a cure for childhood cancer. I was humbled to have the opportunity to speak at the event. I think my speech went off well. My goal was to combine a Shrek impersonation, anecdotes about my terrible dancing and a prison escape, all together with Kylie's story, challenge people to action and make them cry in 9 minutes. It was hard to recover after using the words, "toilet paper" when I meant to say "dental floss." Fortunately, I caught myself and corrected the error.

But it wasn't what I gave to the event that mattered most; it was what I found there.

What I found there was a large group of people affected by cancer and looking for a way to make a difference. *Nobody fights alone.* There were no social, ethnic, economic, or racial distinctions whatsoever – cancer doesn't respect the things that divide society. CureFest brought us together into the tangled mess we are.

Everyone was vulnerable. Everyone was real. I have come to like real.

Sunday afternoon I walked around and met several people I have only known digitally since we started this journey. I also met many new sojourners. Two encounters stand out. One was with a man named Miguel who lost his son, Jonathan, around the same time Kylie died. Miguel is hurting – like I am hurting. His eyes were red the minute we shook hands, and he began telling me about his boy. All I could do was listen, and at some point, I just hugged him – for a long time. You know what? It wasn't weird at all. It didn't feel wrong. It felt perfectly right. I don't think it solved anything for Miguel, but maybe he knows he isn't alone in his pain. Being alone stinks.

Later in my trek, I stumbled upon a man named John who lost his beautiful daughter, Juliana, two years ago from the same cancer that claimed Kylie. In fact, I was told this was the anniversary of her death. Anniversaries are hard. No words, nothing to say… I've learned that much. I just reached out and hugged him and I began to weep. He actually held it together better than I did.

Maybe a lesson I'm learning in all of this is that dropping some barriers and hugging a man is all a part of this vulnerability thing. It actually won't kill me! I might even be the better for it.

So, I hug. I'm a hugger. I hugged Chris, Jonathan, Tony and Peter. Although I am a poor substitute, these men can no longer hug their

Mathias, Alexis, Cole and Mattie like I can't hug Kylie. Did I miss you? I'm around. I'll be back, big boy. I am equal opportunity; I will hug men and women (DISCLAIMER – I am allowed to hug women when and only when my lovely wife deems it appropriate and the hug's duration is less than 3.7 seconds).

Now if I get to Europe someday and a man wants to kiss me on both cheeks, I might recoil a little. I'm not sure Eddie is ready for that.

Glaring Weakness is My Strength

October 28, 2015

I spent the weekend at my college homecoming with the friends of my youth. We were young bucks together – brothers, champions of the field and in the ladies' hearts. True legends of the university, soon to conquer the world. At least that's how we remember it.

Back then, the talk was of girls, sports, parties, and well… girls. This time we mostly talked of the good old days, recent medical procedures, new aches, chronic pains, and family. Our waists are bigger and our hairlines have shifted. Every one of us is slower but wiser. I found it hysterical to go to dinner in this college town when no one had to mooch because we actually have money.

It was so good to see these guys. They have faithfully followed my family's journey through cancer and the loss of Kylie and been a great source of encouragement to me. I needed this weekend to thank them, hug them, be with them and reconnect. This is the first time I've been able to go. Life got in the way for far too long.

I can't tell you how many times one of my old friends told me how much they admire my strength. I'm humbled by that statement… humbled and slightly embarrassed. I have heard it before and I want to let you in on a little secret:

I'm the weakest guy you know.

- I'm not strong unless strength is simply resisting the urge to stay in a fetal position all day long.

- I argue that strength is not the mere act of putting one foot after the other, staggering like a drunk with no foreseeable direction.

- There is no strength in speaking or writing about the little girl I miss so much – that is only desperation, if anything. I am desperate to make sure she isn't blotted out from my feeble memory or yours.

I saw strength – strength that fought the beast to the very end armed with nothing more than a smile. This strength you think you see in me is an illusion. It is more fear than strength. And I will tell you what I tell anyone who gives me that compliment:

You would do the same thing.

If you were faced with the same dilemma and your son or daughter were stuck in a hospital bed, you would do whatever necessary to move one hour into the next. You would do anything for one smile. If you had to shepherd your family past a devastating loss, you would do the same things I have done, probably better. I pray you never have to do so, because then you will know what weakness truly is.

I had downloaded several podcast for the trip. On the way home, I chose a series from *Your Move with Andy Stanley*, who does both leadership podcasts and sermons. I freely admit that I thought this selection was more about leadership because I have steered clear of most preaching since February. The series was about being stuck in circumstances that seem to leave no way out. Very relevant, but he got me – it was taken straight out of the Bible. I listened anyway and the verse that hit me was 2 Corinthians 12:9

My grace is sufficient for you, for my strength is made perfect in weakness. *"* (NKJV)

Since I've been embarrassed about being called strong when I feel so weak, I had to pause the sound and ponder that one. It only took a minute for me to realize that what people see in my weakness is a reflection of perfect strength – but it isn't me! That is a mirage. No, somehow my ineptitude and weakness mirrors the potent strength of an all-powerful God. And aren't I an unlikely surface? With my flaws, dirt, and cracks it would seem impossible to see a reflection at all – much less his!

How does this work? Especially now. Now, in this time where I doubt God, I fear God, and I question God more than at any other time in my life, he somehow uses me now to show himself strong. This is the mystery of God. Like so many things I've encountered in the recent past, there is no explaining him. There is also, at times, no understanding him.

But please understand this: I am weak. I don't know where I'm going. I have no idea what to do. I move forward only because I am compelled to move away from the pain behind me. This is weakness.

Glaring weakness is my strength.

Thankful? (Or Not)

November 26, 2015

My nephew-in-law, JP, is in the poultry business. Usually here in the south, we just drop the formalities and welcome a boy into the family with the "nephew" title as soon as the vows are spoken. But not JP – he's the nephew-in-law. I'm keeping him at arms' length for now because I'm mad at him.

You see, being in the poultry business, last summer JP heard about a coming avian flu scare and warned us that we'd better buy our holiday turkeys before the prices went through the ceiling. The industry was forecasting shortages, rationing, and all kinds of mayhem for November – he said. And this is where we ran afoul of each other. With my entrepreneurial spirit, I loaded up. Thinking that when housewives all over the south were clamoring for turkey that they couldn't get, I would open my friendly freezer door and sell them turkeys at three or four times what I paid. Only the price hikes never came. There was no run on turkey, and yes, my basement freezer contains 500 pounds of bird that is worth no more than when I bought them. I don't even like turkey.

I am currently not thankful for JP.

To be honest, this year has brought me a host of things for which I am NOT thankful. As I consider our Thanksgiving tradition of going around the table and naming something we are thankful for, I wonder what I will say. How will I ignore the empty chair? I am not thankful that Kylie will be absent this Thursday, and I feel that saying I am thankful for something that remains diminishes how supremely unthankful I am for what has been taken. Just like any thanks I could give for JP minimizes the plethora of turkey in my freezer.

No, God, I am not thankful this year.

My mind conjures the image of an old southern preacher with a booming voice, white wispy hair, and thin fingers. He alternates pointing at me with pounding the pulpit as he rattles from the book of Job, *"The Lord giveth, and the Lord taketh away."*

Giving... Taking... I think we humans look for things to be fair, to stay in balance – or at least come close. Most people don't legitimately foresee a windfall in their future, but they don't anticipate losing it all either. The average man just wants to win a few more than he loses and have a little fun along the way. But this loss of Kylie – it can't be balanced. I see no way God can **giveth** equal to what he **tooketh**.

You're going to have to help me with this one, God, because I don't know how to be thankful for what I've been given this year when so much has been lost.

You might read this and wonder how I could feel that way. How could I allow my grief to overshadow the abundant blessings for which I should be thankful? To that I respond with something I learned early in my marriage. It took years for my patient wife to drum into my head the fact that I had no right to tell her how to feel. So I say to you what I was repeatedly told, "Don't tell me how to feel!"

But even while I *feel* decidedly not thankful, I do *see* some things:

I see friends and family who have been our strength and support since our cancer journey began.

I see an abundance of new friends – people who have shared this terrible sadness with me and lived it themselves. While diamonds are formed through time and pressure, friendships can be forged with either. When I meet a parent who has fought childhood cancer, we have an immediate bond. When they have endured loss such as mine, we have an unbreakable one.

I see children who are winning their fight against cancer.

I see my daughters, who not only loved their dying sister with everything they had, but made straight A's, honor roll, and dean's list in the process. How is that possible? Only because they are all three remarkable. If my work over the year had been graded it would have been a marginal D-, at best.

I see a wife who gets up every day, pushes through pain and loss, and loves us completely.

I see a God who has provided abundantly in so many ways. I often feel his love, even while I question it in the next breath. He has made my table full, despite the hole in my heart and empty chair.

I see a new calling and opportunities to engage in the future.

I see a fight we have to win.

I see many good things. And yet, it is still hard to feel thankful.

Maybe your Thanksgiving brings similar emotions. Have you a loss or heartache in your life that leaves you less than thankful? You and I may wrestle with God for the rest of our days. My faith is often stretched to its limit when I consider this: I believe he had the power to change our course and yet chose not to. I will never understand that. In this life I do not believe I will find a patch that mends or a balm that soothes, but I am learning that *people* will bring out thankfulness. Love is all and it is not found in isolation. It is found among others.

So if I can stumble my way to thankfulness this year, it will be for you people. In fact, you might be the only thing I can raise in thanks this year...

Oh, and... do any of you want some turkey?

A Hard Christmas

December 16, 2015

My family is separated by roughly 600 miles. When it came time to leave the nest, my sister went west while I came south. During the past two years, we have enjoyed a rekindled relationship, as I am sure is common when a family member sails turbulent seas. Tragedy has a way of stripping away the veneer of the inconsequential and revealing that of true worth. Family, friends, love, goodness, joy, fellowship – those are things of significance.

We quit exchanging Christmas gifts between adults long ago and focus on the children instead. I once came upon a toy so loud and obnoxious that I knew her home was incomplete without it. It was an ambulance that screamed, "In an emergency, dial 911" at an outrageous decibel. I considered it my service to her. My nephew could barely talk at the time, but after he got the present from Cool Uncle Mark, he certainly knew who to call if mommy took a fall down the stairs. That gift paved the way for cash-only Christmases.

It never seemed like a big deal until this year. I suggested to my lovely wife that instead of sending cash through the mail, we could put money under the tree for our children and they could do the same for theirs. The problem didn't hit me until she said, "We would still have to send them $20."

Why?

They've got four kids; we've got... we've got...

Oh yeah... We've got three.

We used to have four.

Christmas is hard.

Christmas is like a tumbler full of mirth at its finest. When family and friends come home to celebrate the cheer of the season, you drink to your heart's content and are filled by its warming sway.

When you are hurting, the tumbler has a jagged edge. Your attempts to avoid the broken glass often fail, and you are forced to drink your cheer from the chipped side of the cup. You can still get the expected, pure taste of joy, but you might cut your lip taking it in. Other partygoers with intact glasses assume that it is easy to spot the barb before letting it touch your mouth, but often it slips past your sight and the holiday warmth is replaced by the metallic taste of blood.

I knew getting decorations up this year would be hard. I also knew we would run into special items that brought Kylie's sweet face to mind. I was prepared to be sad when the carousel, large plastic Pooh, and her ornaments were unpacked. The Santa hat she wore for years was bound to cause a tear, and her stocking makes me pause each time I pass.

But there have been so many holiday surprises – *jagged edges*.

For instance, it always took two vehicles to get our Christmas tree. I would have it loaded in my truck which only seats five, while mom hauled the kids in the minivan. This year as I walked to the truck expecting to be alone, I noticed the rest of the family following me. While I was surprised, they had done the math and knew we would all fit.

I hated doing the elf on the shelf thing! I hated it with a passion… yet now I miss it so badly.

I didn't like tiptoeing around the Santa issue either. You have to be bright to keep a secret of that magnitude, and I have never been accused of luminosity. Over the years I let slip so many stupid things that nearly gave the whole thing away. We made the decision to let our children be children and believe as long as possible… even if one quite possibly got to high school unsure. At last check, Kylie believed and thought people who didn't believe were just wrong. Never one to be judgmental, our little elf was okay with other people being wrong, if that's what they chose.

A typical December 23rd would find us scrambling for the final presents. We joined Amazon Prime one year because it was the only way to get Christmas delivered on time. The fact that this year we were done shopping on December 8th should be a good thing. Only it isn't. It simply reminds us that was have a quarter fewer presents to buy.

Christmas cards. Such loving reminders of people who care about us. Our mailbox is full every day. In years past, the cards of impressive families were delivered in early December while ours were almost always a kind of New Year's surprise. I do enjoy the cards. But now when I see their smiling faces, all I can see is complete families whereas ours is not. Don't stop sending them – this is a "me" thing, not a "you" thing. Forgive us, though. There will not be a reciprocal card from us this year.

Gatherings are nearly impossible. I want people to have a Merry Christmas. I really do! But being surrounded by joy at a party is nearly suffocating. I've never be claustrophobic, but I can now imagine what the overwhelming urge to break out of a confined space feels like.

I know I am not the only one hurting at the holidays.

As I have considered this aching I have for Kylie, I have stumbled upon four truths about Christmas this year that I would like to share with others who are hurting, grieving, or lonely.

1. Christmas will be hard.

2. You aren't alone in your hurting.

3. Sitting in a fetal position crying doesn't change truth number 1, it just gets uncomfortable.

4. December 26th will come.

So let us raise our glasses to the smooth side and drink in every bit of Christmas joy we can scrape together, knowing that the decorations will soon come down and maybe, just maybe, next Christmas will hold a bit more merriment.

God Bless and Merry Christmas.

Tears in My Stocking

December 25, 2015

What did Santa bring you?

This might be the first Christmas in my life where his visit brought me tears. I don't blame the big guy – he's really got nothing to do with it. He didn't set his elves to build them in his shop, pack them in his bag, or stow them on his sleigh. Santa is like a magnifying glass for all things joyful, and when that joy is lost, he magnifies its absence as well.

I'm sitting here in our den alone at 7 am, drinking my coffee and watching the sun peek through the trees. This could have never happened before. Any other year, I would have been up for over an hour, yawning and probably scratching my backside after staying up well into the night assembling toys and applying stickers. For the past eighteen or so Christmases, there has been too much excitement bubbling and brewing to sleep this late. The girls always sent a messenger to our bedroom to let us know that they were awake, a fact that couldn't slip past us as we listened to feet on stairs and a chorus of giggles. The presents in our den would be covered in bedsheets so prying little eyes wouldn't see what Santa brought. Nice of him to keep that tradition today, even though all I hear from their rooms is snoring.

When I got out here this morning, there were two stockings up: Mom's and Kylie's. I filled Mom's and set it with the others, leaving just one. We have been entertained over the past few days by watching videos of Christmases past. On one, there was a point in the morning carnage where one of the girls noticed a stocking that hadn't been touched, and Daddy Santa had one of those "oh crap" moments before he admitted that he forgot. Mommy Santa didn't forget. She never forgets.

I am sad that my children are past the Santa age. This change was inevitable, but we had a year or two stolen from us. I love the Christmas morning energy, excitement, and wonder. That is just pure, unbridled joy. We could certainly use more of that.

I am also sad that Kylie's stocking is still hung by the chimney with care.

It is not full. It is as empty as her room, her chair, and that chamber of my heart where she used to reside. She will not be dancing up our stairs from the basement where she slept with her sisters on Christmas Eve. I won't get to see her wide smile and starlit gaze. I miss her so much right now that I'm just about ready to push Santa's fat butt up the chimney with his cookie-stained beard and magnifying glass....

... or maybe I should go wake up the troops and see if we can find a smile that will soak up a couple of the tears that the fat elf brought. It is nearly 8 now and I figure there's got to be some joy around here somewhere. I think this year, we might have to search for it.

Merry Christmas!

May you all find joy, even if you have to look high and low for it.

Updated 9:16 am – I woke them up – joy found.

Repurpose

I wonder if ants have names or can tell each other apart. When they form their lines and begin marching, do they have a predetermined order or destination? They always seem to have a purpose. If you have ever put your foot in their way to stop their progress, you will know that they don't stand still, rub their chins disconcertedly, or hold an impromptu meeting to vote on a direction. No, they turn right or left and keep moving as if it had been their plan all along.

Sometimes, you just have to move to avoid being still.

When Kylie's radiation treatment started in Charlotte, she and her mother (along with her grandparents) drove up every Monday and returned on Friday. We all three knew it was the best option – likewise, we knew the separation would be hard. The worst part about being a parent of a cancer patient is being a spectator to their suffering. When her chemo was here at least I could watch, hold, and support. During those four days every week, the separation was more brutal than I ever imagined.

I needed a project and one presented itself. Kylie informed us that when her leg worked again, she wanted to take stage dancing lessons. This gave me an idea to finish a room in the basement with a raised dance floor so that she could practice. We had acquired a pool table long ago that could share the space, so construction began.

I love building. The work occupied my time and my mind while Kylie was gone. When they arrived home for the weekends, I would shut the doors and she never knew. I started to get so excited about the impending surprise.

Then a giant foot slammed down and changed our direction. Unlike a line of ants changing direction, our line stopped completely. Kylie died. She wouldn't need a 12' by 12' dance floor because she attained a celestial ballroom of unlimited proportions.

Construction halted on the room. I stopped moving.

I'm a little dense, but at some point a few months later, it dawned on me that one of Kylie's sisters is a dancer and could profit from the space. I started thinking that if I would build it for Kylie, I should build it for JB – I am no less her daddy. With that in mind, I started moving again. I didn't "move on" – I will never move on. But I did start moving.

The room went from a tap studio to a ballet studio where JB could practice.

The room got **_repurposed_**.

It certainly has a Kylie flair with the yellow, but its purpose is ballet (and occasionally billiards).

There are some very special things in this room I would like to share:

A show poster from *Newsies* that she got to see and six from our Broadway trip after her death.

A painting done by Paige O'Hara (The voice of Belle) for Kylie.

Posters from shows in which she and her sisters have appeared.

Art that was made for her and a couple of pieces she made.

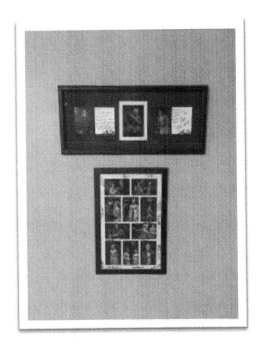

Autographs from the *Aladdin* leads and the *Sense & Sensibility* cast.

Signed picture from her class and my article from Beta Magazine.

And the *piece de resistance:*

The costume made for her to wear in *Aladdin* – given to us by the amazing people at Disney Theatrical.

I love this room! It simply breathes Kylie. But it now serves a different purpose than its original intent.

Like the room, I've been **repurposed**. I thought my life was headed one way until the foot slammed down and pushed me in another direction. Ants may have contingencies and predetermined directions, but I don't. I admit that I don't know exactly where this repurposed life is going. I do know that moving again feels so much better than standing still contemplating my loss.

I'm Glad I Danced

January 12, 2016

Friday held our school's annual Father-Daughter Dance. I am guessing I attended ten of them with different combinations of daughters. There were a few years when all four were in school that I had to call in reinforcements – my brother-in-law and nephews. *A Man Can Only Dance with so Many Women.* (Autobiography title – I call it!)

Most of the dads at our school participate, and I'm proud of that. There are a few who only use the dance floor as a path to the buffet, but they are the exception. Men who may refuse to dance with their wives break out every move they can muster at the twinkle-eyed request of their little girls. If you judged the event on performance, it isn't pretty. If you judge it by love, it is beautiful.

We've all heard the song "I Hope You Dance." Its lyrics contain such a good message. I don't claim to have done everything right or been wonder-dad, but I danced.

I'm glad I danced.

Friday evening, my lovely wife opened Facebook and saw friends posting pictures of dads and daughters headed to the dance. She quickly closed it. She didn't want to see it. I get that. After all, I don't have a date in what should have been Kylie's last dance. That stings. But somehow, I didn't mind seeing the pics scroll by. In fact, I kind of enjoyed them. I think I didn't mind because I danced.

I'm glad I never let my inability dictate my participation.

I'm glad I never sat out because I might be embarrassed of what others thought.

I'm glad I danced.

Can I dance, you ask? The answer is a resounding no. In my younger days, I was never asked to return to the floor by sane, sober women, and I will likely never be part of a hokey flash mob at one of my girl's weddings. (There are two reasons for that. First, my girls won't want that to be what the attendees remember of their wedding. Secondly, we probably won't be able to afford the space required to ensure the safety of the guests. I think the Fire Marshall requires about three square miles of covered space per Mark Myers Turn.)

Still, I'm glad I danced.

I'm glad I let my girls put bows in my hair and makeup on my face. I am also glad Facebook, Instagram, and digital photography weren't prolific a decade ago.

Of course I wish I had been able to dance Friday with Kylie, who should be eleven months out of treatment and sporting new hair. Last year, she couldn't stay very long because she was aching all over. On the ride home we talked about how much fun this year would be. We thought her pain was the accumulated side effects of radiation. In retrospect, we now know that it was the cancer creeping throughout her body. Still we danced. For however long we could, we danced.

Maybe that is why I wasn't affected by seeing the other dads taking their girls to the dance – because I danced… because I have no regrets.

To young or future fathers of girls: DANCE. Dance like every turn might be the last, because it actually might be. I don't say that to be morose, I say it because it is true. None of us are promised another tomorrow, and the quicker we realize that, the better off our today will be. Steal joy from every moment; live with no regrets.

DANCE

Run, Daddy, Run

January 27, 2016

I decided to put a purpose behind the first four marathons I ran. I chose a daughter for each and focused on that one during my long training runs and even on race day. I called them prayerathons – but not out-loud because that sounds really cheesy and cliché.

To take things a step further, I asked each one of them to draw a picture for me to have printed on the back of my race shirt, and I gave them the race medal. Here are the first three:

Meredith- Grumpy

Kendall – Phineas & Ferb

Jenna made a tie-dye

All are very special, but the final one has become incredibly dear to me. Kylie was six when it was her turn. The Birmingham Marathon was nine days before her seventh birthday, and she decided to draw penguins for me since they were her favorite animal. As I have mentioned in the past, she was very meticulous about her drawing, and the slightest mistake would require a redo. She threw out many subpar penguins in her quest for perfection. Finally, she came up with this:

When she gave it to me, she explained with a kiss on the nose that I was to "Run, daddy, run. Then waddle home to me."

That became my purpose for the race and I did just that. I ran one of my best times, and anyone who has run a marathon can attest, waddling is what you do afterwards.

I've thought about that a lot since her death.

What is my purpose?

What do I want to do now?

What race have I been entered into because of cancer? That entry fee was astronomically high.

At some point it dawned on me that she set my life's course those many years ago. Her drawing wasn't merely about that marathon, it is about the current race of life I'm running.

Like any marathon, I just have a run my best to the finish line and then waddle home to her.

I run by telling her story.

I run by showing others how they can have joy during any storm.

I run by preaching the need for safer and more effective cures for childhood cancer.

I run by sharing the Jesus that Kylie knew and the faith she wouldn't relinquish even until she saw his face.

I run that way until that day when my time in this world is done and I waddle home to her.

And when I get weary, I stop at a water station to refresh myself before finding the strength to set out once more. There is no retirement in this race. I may be at mile 14 right now or mile 25 – I have no way of knowing. I do know that this is my course, set forth by the strongest person I ever knew when she was but six years old.

I will run...

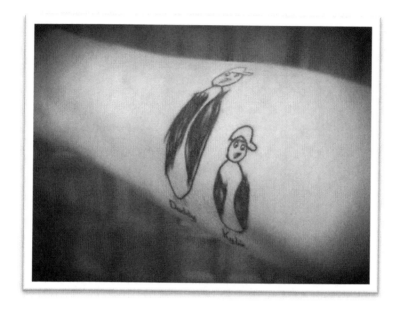

...then waddle home to her.

I Don't Want to Share This

February 7, 2016

I know we didn't talk much because we were both wrapped up in our own nightmares, but I wanted to tell you about a vague memory I have – probably one of the earliest burned in my brain. It must have been around 1973 because I was at prime lesson-learning age for a boy. My friend, Tommy, was over, and we decided to play marbles. You looked a lot younger than me. So, in case you don't know, those are spherical objects you must manipulate with your hands for entertainment because they have no electronics embedded inside. I know, sounds primitive.

The problem was that I'd been given a taw by my grandfather and Tommy wanted to use it. Back off, pal! My little self had no intention of sharing that new marble – it was way too special to be touched by someone else's grubby mitts. This didn't set well with Tommy, and a fight ensued that spilled over into the hall and eventually into the kitchen where my mother was cooking. My mother did not appreciate my selfishness.

Knowing I was in trouble, I closed my hand over the marble and shoved my fist in my pocket. An inquisition began during which Tommy truthfully laid out everything. For my part, wrong or not, I was stubborn enough to keep my clenched fist in my pocket, and the two of them weren't strong enough to wrangle it out. Frustrated, Tommy left and my mother gave me one more chance to give her the marble. I refused. My course was set. I had not yet been convinced of the propriety of sharing. When my father came home, I was enlightened – not only about sharing, but about respecting my mother. I am fairly certain I ate my dinner standing up that evening.

I have been married long enough that I share pretty well now. I do grimace if anyone wants to use one of my tools or even set foot in my shop. But most of the time, I get over it. I also have an issue with the console of my truck. I really don't want to share that space even with my wife's little lipstick tube. I don't know why.

This may sound rude, but I have something I don't want to share with you. I will hold this tightly in my closed palm and do everything I can to keep you from seeing or touching it. I don't want to share it with you. In fact, I would lock it in a vault, hire security and do nearly anything to keep you from it – because it is simply unbearable.

I don't want to share this with you.

I don't want you to know what it is to yearn for the return of something you can't have.

I don't want you to live in the past because the present only brings pain and regret.

I don't want you to lie hour after hour staring at a dark ceiling because you can't turn off your mind long enough to sleep.

I don't want you to look into the tear-stained eyes of your wife, wondering if she will ever smile again.

I would do anything to keep this from you.

I don't want you to have to tell your precious child that they are going to die and watch as they process the information.

I don't want you to say goodbye, that you will see them again someday in another place. Likewise, I don't want you to yearn for the hastening of that day because this life without them is too hard.

I don't want you to smell the dirt of your child's freshly dug grave.

I don't want to share this burden of guilt as a father and husband – guilt like a thick winter coat buttoned and zipped so tightly you cannot remove it, whether it is justified or not.

I don't want to share this with you.

I will buy you a thousand marbles and even give you the special taw I withheld. I don't even know you, and I would do anything in my power to keep this away from you – not to share this thing...

But if we must share it, we will shoulder it together and do everything within our power to keep our fists in our pockets so that no one else has to join us... Deal?

Dear Kylie,

February 10, 2016

I can't believe it's been almost a year since we said goodbye. Since I held you in my arms and carried you out of the house. To say I miss you is an understatement. I think about you every day. I wonder what you would be like now, almost fourteen. I wonder if your hair would have come back curly. I know you didn't want that. You just wanted your hair to be like it was before cancer. You just wanted to be normal.

I'm sorry you got cancer. I need you to know that I didn't lie to you when we talked about winning. I always believed we would. It never crossed my mind that you would die. Maybe it's stupid to be optimistic about stuff, I don't know. We all have different outlooks on life and mine is a little like Pollyanna… or Paddington. Remember how I read his books to you and Jenna at bed time? Paddington always thought the best of situations and people, even of Mr. Curry. Maybe I'm like that simple, stuffed bear.

From the very beginning, I thought we would win. Even on your very last morning when I prayed in the basement, I believed God would change it. I don't understand why he didn't. I've asked him but he doesn't answer. I prayed so hard that he would make you well or take me instead. Wouldn't healing you have been the best way to let this world know he was still around? It's the story I would have written. If there's one thing I've learned in this whole mess, it is that I don't hold the pen.

Sometimes I feel like I'm stuffed in this big, black bag that he gets to shake around, but I'm sealed off inside so he doesn't have to hear me when I scream. I know it isn't right, but it is how I feel and no one gets to tell me how to feel (I learned that from your mommy). It's just so weird thinking about God now. It's like he is a million miles away one minute and so close I can't see past him the next. If you run into him today up there, tell him I'm not mad at him. I just don't understand his plan and why you had to go to him and not stay with me. No, I'm not mad, but I am actually a little afraid of him. Of course, he'll probably just laugh and say it is right for me to be afraid. He is God, after all.

Christmas was lame without you. Nobody here believes anymore; you were the last one who still thought… **Oops!** I've said too much. But I guess you know by now. December was a double whammy of missing you and the loss of Christmas magic. We still put the tree out and hung your stocking and all of your special ornaments. I still complained about hauling the decorations up and down the stairs. Some things never change.

I'll finish this letter soon and you might get some letters from other friends. They say it helps a person grieve to write a letter like this, but I don't know about that. I'm not sure anything really helps. My heart has a Kylie-sized hole that no amount of paper can patch.

You and me for always,

Daddy

Dear Kylie (Part 2),

February 12, 2016

Dear Kylie,

Tomorrow marks a year since you left. I miss you so bad it hurts. I hope you have had time to read all of the beautiful letters people wrote to you. It isn't just me and your family who miss you. You left a ginormous hole for a fairly small girl.

Since we can't have you here with us, we watch videos of you all the time. We have our favorites. *Annie* is one, of course. Also, we laughed and laughed about the Disney cruise when you missed mommy and wouldn't stay at the kids' camps. Our little pager said: *Kylie would like to be picked up at Monstro Point* and *Kylie would like to be picked up at Animator's Pallet.* When I interviewed you to see what your favorite parts of the day were, I asked you what you did when you didn't want to stay and you said, "Um, cwied." There was no remorse in your little voice.

"Um, cwied" is our family catchphrase now.

I'm kind of nervous to tell you this next part. I've got two tattoos – okay three but I'm not counting the little dot I got to show it you didn't hurt when you had to get marked for radiation. You let me get that one! I know you would be mortified and I'm sorry. One is the Smiley for Kylie logo, and the other is the penguin picture you drew me for the marathon. You told me to "run Daddy, run, then waddle home to me." I'm trying to run. I figure the best way to run is to keep on telling people about you – your faith, your joy, and the cancer that we need to kill. Someday I will waddle home to you, and I'm kind of ready for that. Does that sound weird – that I'm kind of sick of this place and ready to see you again? It's true. Nothing is the same without you. I'm not going to jump in front of a bus anytime soon, but I would be the first to push someone out of the way.

I did go ahead and run the marathon that I was training for before you died. Okay, I walked a lot. My worst time by far, but I finished. I still run so I don't turn into fat daddy again, but not as far as I used to. I'm spending most of my time writing.

I'm finally releasing the last Virgil Creech book that we started reading together. I think it's pretty good – I wish you had gotten to finish it. I wonder if you just know how it ends since you are up there. Hey, if there's a library, can you get it in for me? Maybe stash it in Charles Dickens' backpack when he's not looking?

I'm glad I finished that because mostly I write about YOU now! My blog gets a lot more readers (when you are the subject), and I am working on a book about things you did to take back your joy from cancer. I think it could help people who have to go through hard times like you did. *Sometimes I can only smile because you taught me how.* You showed me that every minute is precious and joy can be unearthed anywhere if you dig deep enough. You were chock full of amazing.

Oh, Kylie. I miss you so much. I know I said it before, but it's true. I miss seeing your smile and hearing your giggle. I miss watching you perform. We went to Broadway, but it wasn't the same without you. You got your Broadway debut, though! It should have been on a stage, but it was on a billboard instead. Lots of people saw it. You are making a difference.

I guess I just wanted to say I love you, I miss you, I'm sorry, and I will never forget you. You are the inspiration for everything I do from now until that glorious day when I get to hold you again.

You and me for always,

Daddy

Dear Kylie… Love, Meredith

February 13, 2016

Dear Kylie,

I remember standing in the wings during my high school production of *Little Women* and shedding a tear when Jo and Beth said the lines: "When you were first born, not an hour old, I told Marmee, 'Beth is mine!'"

My favorite memory has always been the day you were born. Maybe that day has always been so infinitely dear to me because you're the only sister I remember welcoming into the world. In fact, I recently found the birthday card I made for you that first day, which read: "Dear Kylie, How do you like the world? Love, Meredith." When I remember that day, it's not just a faded memory of child May May that I tease myself about (as you know I so often do). It is one of the memories that I can relive most vividly. I genuinely feel the six-year-old excitement, so simple and pure and all consuming, when I stumbled out of bed to find Grandmama and Granddaddy in the living room. I recall the way my heart leapt for joy when they told me that I had a new sister, and she decided to come a day early. I can hear the pitter patter of my bare feet across the kitchen floor when the first thing I did when I heard the news was run as fast as I could to the kindergarten calendar in order to make sure to move your "Happy Birthday" sticker to the appropriate date. I feel that same pride I felt when Kendall and Jenna got bored at the hospital (understandably so, at 4 years old and 18 months), and I got to stay with you while Grandmama and Granddaddy drove them home. I felt so much pride that day: I was the big sister. I was the one who stayed. Mommy and Daddy even let me help to choose your middle name. I don't think my little heart knew what to do with how much joy I felt holding you for the first time, and knowing that I was going to help take care of you, that I got to watch you grow, and help you learn, and be your friend. I know exactly what Jo meant when she said, "Beth is mine!" On that very first day, even at the age of 6, I claimed: "Kylie is mine!"

Jo went on: "Everyone has someone special in the world, and I have you, my sweet Beth."

We had that conversation daily. Every day, even sometimes more than once a day, I made sure to tell you, "I love you more than anything in the world, do you know that?" and you always said "Yes, and I love you most." You always jumped to most so we wouldn't have to go back and forth with the "more's." And I always looked up to how you wouldn't say, "I love you more than anything in the world" back to me. It wasn't that you didn't love me enough to make such drastic statements, it was that you had your priorities straight, and even though you loved me so very much, I know that you didn't want to say you loved me more than God or the rest of the family. You were so sincere. And I sincerely meant to make a statement that drastic, but your heart was just too whole to make comparisons. Your love didn't need to measure up to anything else. There was more than enough to go around.

I still whisper to myself almost daily that I love you more than anything in the world. And then I say a prayer that God will pass along my message.

I distinctly remember feeling a tear roll down my cheek when Jo and Beth proceeded to sing their last duet, and the thought triumphantly marched through my mind: "I could never bear to lose my Beth."

I don't know why God decided that my plan for us was wrong. My plan for us was perfect in my mind: I would get to hear you sing so many more songs and watch you draw so many more beautiful pictures. Even though we're older now, we'd have time for a few more games of Barbie dolls and Disney Princess dress up. We would someday get to be in a show together. You would be my maid of honor. I'd get to see which of your innumerable talents you turned into an enormously successful career. When I had children someday, I'd watch you be the "Awesomest Aunt Kylie," a title that you always predicted you would get to be. I wanted to see you share your abundant love, your overflowing joy, your contagious laughter, and your genuine heart with so many people as we grew old, forever best friends. There was nothing bad in my plan. There was no cancer. There was no sorrow. There was no loss.

I don't know why God's plan didn't show itself to be more like mine. I often have trouble reconciling how to feel about the path He has put us on. And when I grieve or fear or doubt, I remember your sweet voice boldly declaring that if God decided to give you cancer, then "He must have big plans for me."

He had a big plan for you. My heart aches to say that in that plan there has been cancer. There has been sorrow. There has been loss. But I want you to know how incredibly proud of you I have always been, and still am. I want you to know that despite the cancer, the sorrow, and the loss, I did get to see part of my plan in action: your abundant love, your overflowing joy, your contagious laughter, and your genuine heart, all shared so purposefully with so many people. God has used and continues to use you and your story in incredibly powerful ways.

Every day I hope to live a little bit more like you. I've learned so many lessons from you, both in your 13 years with me and since, but I think the most profound lessons you've given to me are the sincere gratitude of knowing that you are in a perfect place where there is no cancer, sorrow, or loss, and the deep thankfulness that comes with the promise that someday I'll get to join you.

I love you more than anything in the world, my sweet Kylie!

—May May

Dear Kylie... Love, Kendall

February 13, 2016

Dear Kylie,

I don't know where to begin. I've wanted to write this for weeks now. I keep putting it off because I know writing it out will hurt, but it hurts anyway. There are so many things I want to say to you because it's been a year. I never thought I'd go an entire year without talking to you and I never wanted to. In fact, this has been the worst year of my life solely because I can't talk to you. I haven't seen your smile or heard your voice in so long, and pictures and videos just aren't the same. I miss you, Kylie, but it's more than that. I missed you when you spent days in the hospital and when you were in Charlotte, but it was never like this. Sometimes I miss you so much my heart physically hurts; I didn't even know that was possible. Too much has changed in the past year. Sometimes I fear you may not recognize me. Before I sat down to write this, I spent four hours with other people by choice! I know you have some joke to make about that, I just wish I could hear it.

Almost daily I think about how you would react to what's going on now. I imagine how happy you'd be that I chose a college only forty minutes from home because I could come back every weekend to see you. I think of what you would say about the stories I tell mom when I come home from school. I spend so much of my time thinking about you that I start to remember things that we did so many years ago without trying to. I remember you coming to sit on my beanbag and forcing me to talk to you because you didn't feel like I had talked to you enough that day. Every once in a while I'll find myself researching the progress on the *Peter and the Starcatchers* movie because you used to ask me to look it up every day (By the way, there has been no progress, and I seriously doubt that it will actually happen.) I remember mornings when you would come to wake me up. You were so loud that you would wake me up before you meant to, so I pretended to be asleep until you crawled up next to me and kissed my cheek. Sometimes I'm not even sure if these things really happened or if I'm imagining them. I hope they're real because every moment I can remember with you in it is precious.

I remember the last few days more and more this time of year. Those are the few memories I wish I could forget. I remember the desperation and denial. The anger and confusion. I remember trying to think about anything else, but I couldn't. I remember the last day when I wished I could switch places with you, but suddenly I realized that was selfish. You fought your fight with cancer and it was time for me, and the rest of the family, to let you go to a better place. Time for us to take our turn with pain and tears. Of course, I wanted you to hold on, but I could never ask you to suffer even more just to spare me pain.

You fought so bravely and it was time for you to have some peace while the rest of us took a turn on the battlefield. Now I just have to learn to live with that.

I miss you. I'll never stop missing you. In your short life you became so much a part of me and I will never change. I wish I could spend even just a little more time with you, but since I can't I'll have to settle for this. Kylie, I hope you know how much I love you and always will even though I can't tell you in person anymore. I ask every night for God to give you the kisses that I can't. I miss your contagious smile, and your great big bear hugs. I miss the way you could always cheer me up. And yes, I even miss your inexplicable ability to get me to do anything you wanted. I love you, Kylie. You are constantly in my thoughts and, more importantly, in my heart. You will always be my baby sister. I love and miss you more than you could ever know.

With all my love,

Kendall

Dear Kylie… Love, Jenna

March 21, 2016

Dear Kylie,

I've been putting off writing this for over a month now. In fact, I almost just didn't do it. The rest of our family is so good with words and the letters they wrote seemed to cover everything. Plus, I'm the science one of the family so I thought I would leave the writing up to them. But then I realized that this is my letter to you, and it doesn't matter if I'm good at writing or not. You would still want to hear from me.

I miss you more than words can describe. Your absence is always present. I will always feel like there is something missing from my life. I miss you coming into my room and hanging out with me. I miss texting you when I was bored. I miss being the "little girls" with you. I often remember games we used to play and things we used to joke. Like when we wrote a whole ballet together or all of our dress-up games.

When we used to play high school, or write songs and choreograph musical numbers together. And of course, all of our Barbie games. The list goes on and on. You were my built-in best friend since the day you were born, and this year without you has been absolutely terrible.

When you passed away, I was mad. I was mad at the doctors for not saving you. I was mad at myself because I couldn't do more to help you. I was mad at God for taking you. I'm still a little mad. I remember when Mom and Dad told me that we only had a few days with you, I cried harder than I thought possible. I remember not being able to breathe. I remember desperately praying for God to heal you. And I remember how you hugged me, kissed my head, and tried to comfort me. I have no idea how you managed to be that strong. I didn't really believe you were going to die. Even during those last few days I thought God was going to show us a miracle, and I was mad when He didn't. Those last days with you were by far the worst days of my life. Unfortunately, I remember them so vividly. The first few weeks you were gone, those days were mostly what I thought about. I hated thinking about them. I didn't want to remember those days. But slowly I started remembering the good times more often than the bad. I started remembering the smiles, the hugs, the cuddles, and all the love and joy that you radiated. I like remembering that a whole lot more. The pain from the memories of your last days with us is still there, and it always will be, but the good memories are starting to be more prominent. I know that is what you would want.

I think about you all of the time. I think of you every morning when I stand next to your sink in our bathroom and when I walk past your bedroom door on the way to mine. I think of you every day when we eat dinner and your chair is empty and whenever I dance in your studio in the basement. I think about you every time I hear music from *Aladdin*. I think about you every time I hold Liza. Sometimes all of these reminders bring tears and pain, but other times they bring back happy memories that make me smile. Even after a year without you, you are still making me smile, Kylie. And I'm not the only one. You have brought smiles to so many people, during your life and after. I think that's absolutely amazing and I know that is something you would be proud of.

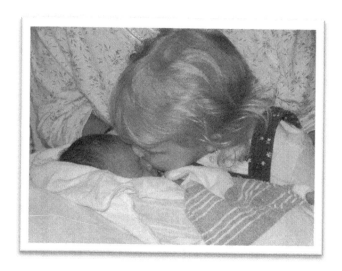

You are still a huge part of my daily life and you always will be. Do you remember when we were little and got matching bracelets that said "Big Sister" and "Little Sister"? We used to wear them all the time. I found them a few months ago and now I wear both of them every day. One of the hardest parts of this year without you has been knowing that I'm not a big sister anymore. I often think about all the times we would have shared. Like how I would have driven you everywhere after I got my license, and we would have sung at the top of our lungs in the car. I really wanted the chance to be the amazing older sister that Meredith and Kendall are to me, and I absolutely hate that I can't be that for you. Little sisters are supposed to look up to their big sisters. However, you went through more than any kid ever should. And you were stronger and wiser beyond your years. I look up to you, Kylie Bug. You are my hero and I try my best to be even a tiny bit like you.

Next year is going to be so hard. I should be driving you to school every morning and hanging out with you there. I shouldn't be the only kid at home. Losing you doesn't seem right or fair. I still don't understand God's plan, and maybe I never will. I might not see how His plan is better than mine, but I am choosing to trust that it is. One thing God has taught me through losing you is that I don't have to be strong enough to get through this on my own. He has shown me that I can always rely on Him to give me the strength to get through the day. I bet that's something He taught you when you were sick. He also gave me a pretty awesome family that will always be there for me when I need them. You would be so proud of them, Kylie! They are all working so hard on that special mission you gave us!

I know you told Mommy to take care of Liza, but I thought you would want to know that I'm taking care of Stan for you. He misses you a lot.

I love you lots, Little Nugget, and I miss you more than you know. I can't wait to play with you again!

Forever your big sister,

Jenna

Dear Kylie... Love, Mommy

February 13, 2016

Dear precious Kylie,

I have thought for weeks about what to say to you; in fact, I've said most of it to you already since I talk to you all the time. The written word has always held a huge place in my life. My career has been words. But ever since you got sick, they have all dried up inside me. It's as if the agony has just been too much, and I haven't really wanted to write it down to stare back at me in the hard reality of black and white.

But here I sit, in a quiet room, without your voice drifting to me from some other part of the house. Without your smile lighting up the room. Without your head nestled on my shoulder. Without your laughter lifting my spirits. Without your hand grasping mine. And even without words, it is all too real.

I can still feel your hand in mine. Sometimes when I am walking I even reach back for your hand. Often in a store I will stop to look at something I think you will like before it hits me all over again. I cried in the aisle of Target the first time I bought pretzels that you wouldn't eat.

Your friends are getting bigger and looking older. I love seeing them, getting hugs, and hearing about what they are doing. But it breaks my heart a little to see them change and wonder what you would look like now. To think about all the things you should be doing with them. I never take a single breath without thinking of you.

I was supposed to be the mommy, Kylie. The one who taught you. But instead, you taught me — about determination, compassion, selflessness, joy, humility, kindness, and friendship (the real kind that costs something to give). You were the first person to reach out to someone who needed a friend. You accepted the lead and the ensemble role with equal grace and gratitude. You followed every rule, did your best on every assignment, brought peace and joy to our home, and lit up every space you entered. And then cancer hit. Then we saw a depth of character in you that defied description. You didn't complain. You didn't get mad at God. You smiled through unimaginable pain. You longed to help other kids suffering like you. You loved us fiercely and battled for every second to spend with us. You are the bravest person I ever met. You are my hero. When I grow up, I want to have as strong a faith and love as well as you did.

I've thought a lot about when you were a baby. Most moms are happy when their babies start sleeping through the night. But I loved getting up to feed you. It was the only time I got to snuggle you and love on you with no interruptions. I'm thankful for every moment in the rocking chair, every single hymn, every single kiss on your cheek.

I loved every single thing about being your mommy, and now that you are no longer here, I sometimes feel like I have forgotten how to live. We spent every single second of those last 10 months together. And I still haven't gotten used to being alone again. I miss reading books together, cuddling, knitting – I finished Noah's blanket for you. It isn't as good as it would have been if you had done it, but he and Lindsay approve. And I tell him often how much you already loved him. I don't know what I would do without videos. Some days I don't think I could survive without hearing your voice and your laugh. Uncle Cary copied lots of our videos for us and we have a bunch of you when you were little. You would have loved watching them with your sisters and me. Every now and then someone sends us a picture we have never seen before. I love that. Each one is a precious gift.

Mostly, I want you to know that you are still as much a vital part of our family as you ever were. You are with us at every meal, in every smile, in every hug. When you continuously found joy in being with the ones you loved even in the worst of times, you didn't realize you were teaching us how to keep going without you. But that is exactly what you were doing. I miss you every single second of every day, but I am savoring each moment with your sisters and Daddy and hugging them tightly for you. You would be so proud of them all. They are loving each other well, taking care of me and continuing to fight this childhood cancer beast on your behalf, but I can see how much they miss you in their eyes.

I am taking good care of Liza, too (Daddy and your sisters tease me that I spoil her rotten), but really she is the one taking care of me. She cuddles with me all the time, and I know it is because you wanted her to. You would have loved watching her grow up. Oh, how I would have loved watching you grow up.

But someday we will be together again. I wouldn't be able to stand it if I didn't know that for certain. While I would have given anything to write this story differently and I honestly can't fathom why God chose to write it this way, I am overcome with gratitude for His gift of redemption and that most glorious promise of forever. Right now it feels like it's been forever without you and it will be forever until I see you again. But the truth is that FOREVER is how long we will be together. So, save me an eternal supply of those brilliant smiles and amazing hugs.

I will love you forever and always,

Mommy

Epilogue

So where do we go from here? I wish I knew. While I compiled and packaged these words into a memoir of our past two years, I am not writing the story. I'm just a minor character in God's design, trying to make something out of the ashes. I do know that I have had a bomb dropped onto my life and I will never be the same.

I feel a calling to share Kylie's story with others through written and spoken word. It is cathartic for me – a way for me to grieve, and in doing so I help to keep her memory alive. But I also believe her story is one that can help others. She developed a very unique way of stealing joy from the horrible situation she was forced to endure. That is a rare trait.

She taught me to take back joy when it seems impossible. I credit her with every smile I can muster through this veil of grief. She also taught me to live every moment with love and kindness. Each day is a gift meant to be devoted to others and given away. Shame on me for living forty-seven years without understanding what my twelve-year-old inherently knew.

Since I became a believer, I have read about the need to die to self in order to learn to live. I never fully understood what that meant until someone I love was taken away. Now my decisions are no longer made based on my benefit. I do things with two overarching goals: to share the message of Christ and to find safer and more effective treatments for childhood cancer.

I don't fear anymore. Who can hurt me now when I am so ready to go and see Kylie? I have developed a true eternal perspective that I was supposed to have anyway. Jesus said:

"Do not be afraid of those who kill the body and after that can do no more." Luke 12:4 (NIV)

It is an odd feeling to live every day free of fear. Since Kylie's death, I am bolder and yet more vulnerable at the same time. This is rarified air out here on this ledge. I've been on mission trips to Haiti and Africa and seen people living this way, and I always thought I would have to give away all of my possessions and become a missionary in the jungle to find this place. If I could change the way I inched out onto the ledge, I would have done it years ago. I can't change the past. I can, however, try to change the future. In light of my own awakening, these things I will do:

I will fight for children with cancer until I hold mine in my arms once more.

I will cherish my family and friends as if every moment together is our last, because I now know it could be.

I will love more and hate less.

I will walk alongside people through their wilderness of no.

I will share the Jesus who carries me when I cannot stand.

I will live with the joy that I learned from a special little girl who I loved as long as I was able.

I will smile through my pain.

If I can help you or your group with any of these things, please contact me through my website: www.markmyers.net or email me at mark@smileyforkylie.com. I would love to share Kylie's story and my experience with you in any way I can.

Appendix

Childhood Cancer Facts

Diagnosis

The incidence of childhood cancer is on the increase, averaging 0.6% increase per year since mid-1970's, resulting in an overall increase of 24% over the last 40 years. (1)

1 in 285 children will be diagnosed with cancer in 2014. (1)

43 children per day or 15,780 children per year are expected to be diagnosed in 2014 with cancer (10,450 ages 0 to 14, and 5,330 ages 15 to 19). (1)

The average age at diagnosis is 6 years old, while adults' average age for cancer diagnosis is 66. (9)

Childhood cancer is not one disease – there are 16 major types of pediatric cancers and over 100 subtypes. (1)

Survival

The average 5-year survival rate for childhood cancers when considered as a whole is 83%. (1, 3)

Cancer survival rates vary not only depending upon the type of cancer, but also upon individual factors attributable to each child. (6)

Survival rates can range from almost 0% for cancers such as DIPG, a type of brain cancer, to as high as 90% for the most common type of childhood cancer known as Acute Lymphoma Leukemia (ALL). (1)

The average survival rate not including children with ALL is 80%. (1)

In 2010 there were 379,112 childhood cancer survivors in the United States. (1)

Approximately 1 in 530 young adults between the ages of 20 years and 39 years is a survivor of childhood cancers. (1)

Pediatric Cancer 5-Year Observed Survival Rates for 2 Time Periods, Ages Birth to 19 Years (1)

The table below contrasts the estimated 5-year survival rates for various types of childhood cancers for the 1975-1979 and 2002-2009 time periods. It should be noted the survival rates listed below reflect general rates and in no way are a representation of an anticipated actual survival outcome for any individual child.

	YEAR OF DIAGNOSIS	
	1975-1979, %	2003-2009,* %
All ICCC sites	63%	83%
Leukemia	48%	84%
Acute lymphocytic leukemia	57%	90%
Acute myeloid leukemia	21%	64%
Lymphomas and reticuloendothelial neoplasms	72%	91%
Hodgkin lymphoma	87%	97%
Non-Hodgkin lymphoma	47%	85%
Brain and CNS	59%	75%
Ependymoma	37%	81%
Astrocytoma	69%	85%
Medulloblastoma	47%	70%
Neuroblastoma and ganglioneuroblastoma	54%	79%
Retinoblastoma	92%	99%
Wilms tumor	75%	90%
Hepatic tumors	25%	74%
Bone tumors	49%	73%
Osteosarcoma	45%	71%
Ewing sarcoma	42%	72%
Rhabdomyosarcoma	49%	64%
Testicular germ cell tumors	74%	96%
Ovarian germ cell tumors	75%	94%
Thyroid carcinoma	99%	98%
Melanoma	83%	95%

CNS indicates central nervous system; ICCC, International Classification of Childhood Cancers.

*Cases were followed through 2010.

Note: Does not include benign and borderline brain tumors.

Source: National Cancer Institute Surveillance, Epidemiology, and End Results (SEER) program, 9 SEER registries.

Long-Term Health Effects Associated
with Treatments & Survival

More than 95% of childhood cancer survivors will have a significant health-related issue by the time they are 45 years of age (2); these health-related issues are side effects of either the cancer, or more commonly, the result of its treatment. 1/3rd will suffer severe and chronic side effects; 1/3rd will suffer moderate to severe health problems; and 1/3rd will suffer slight to moderate side effects. (2)

Mortality

Cancer is the number one cause of death by disease among children. (4)

About 35% of children diagnosed with cancer will die within 30 years of diagnosis. (8)

On average, about 17% of children die within 5 years of diagnosis. Among those children that survive to five years from diagnosis, 18% will die within 30 years of diagnosis. (8)

Those that survive the five years have an eight times greater mortality rate due to the increased risk of liver and heart disease and increased risk for reoccurrence of the original cancer or of a secondary cancer. (8)

There are 71 potential life years lost on average when a child dies of cancer, compared to 17 potential life years lost for adults. (1)

Treatment, Research, Funding

Since 1980, only three drugs, two used in the treatment of ALL, teniposide (1980) (6) and clofarabine (2004) (7), and Unituxin (dinutuximab), recently approved in March, 2015 (7) for use in high risk neuroblastoma, have been approved in the first instance for use in children, and only four more new drugs have been approved for use by both adults and children. Since 1980, fewer than 10 drugs have been developed for use in children with cancer — including those specifically for children and those for both children and adults – compared with hundreds of drugs that have been developed specifically for adults. Equally important, for many of the childhood cancers, the same treatments that existed in the 1970's continue without change as of 2014. (10)

The average cost of a stay in a hospital for a child with cancer is $40,000 per stay. (5)

On average, pediatric hospitalizations for cancer cost almost five times as much as hospitalizations for other pediatric conditions. (5)

For 2014, the National Cancer Institute (NCI) budget is $4.9 billion. It is anticipated that childhood cancer will receive 4% of that sum, or $195 million. (7)

Prostate cancer (patient average age at diagnosis, 66 years), receives more research funding from NCI than all childhood cancers (patient average age at diagnosis, 6 years). (7) (1)

References

1. American Cancer Society, Childhood and Adolescent Cancer Statistics, 2014

2. St. Jude Children's Research Hospital, (JAMA. 2013:309 [22]: 2371-2381)

3. American Cancer Society: Declining Childhood and Adolescent Cancer Mortality, Cancer 2014

4. National Vital Statistics Report, vol. 62.6, December 20, 2013

5. Healthcare Cost and Utilization Project (HCUP), Statistical Brief #132, Pediatric Cancer Hospitalizations 2009

6. American Society of Clinical Oncology

7. The National Cancer Institute

8. CureSearch.org Cancer Statistics

9. Additional information in this statement was obtained from several reliable and authoritative sources

THIS DOCUMENT IS NOT INTENDED TO OFFER SPECIFIC STATISTICS REGARDING AN INDIVIDUAL PATIENT OR THE PATIENT'S SPECIFIC FORM OF CANCER AND IS NOT A SUBSTITUTE FOR INFORMATION THAT MAY BE SOUGHT FROM A PHYSICIAN. IT IS MERELY INTENDED, BASED ON INFORMATION PRESENTLY AVAILABLE TO THE AUTHORS, TO BE A GOOD FAITH GENERAL PRESENTATION OF CHILDHOOD CANCER STATISTICS THAT MAY BE HELPFUL TO OTHERS SEEKING SUCH GENERAL INFORMATION.

These statistics come from The Truth 365 and have been used with permission. For more information, please visit: www.thetruth365.org

The Purpose of Smiley for Kylie

This purpose statement was written with Kylie to keep us focused and let others know what we were doing. Kylie often reminded us that everything hinged on number one: to bring glory to God.

Kylie was diagnosed with Ewing's Sarcoma on April 9, 2014. Soon after, we started Smiley for Kylie as a way of smiling for her when she couldn't because of cancer. We envisioned friends and family using it to uplift our girl. Little did we know that it would spread as far as it has. Here is what Kylie and I created and called our Purpose Statement of Smiley for Kylie.

Smiley for Kylie exists for four reasons:

1. To make God Smile – Philip Yancey said, *"Endurance is not just the ability to bear a hard thing, but to turn it to glory."* * Through even this nightmare, we hope to point others to the God we know.

2. To make Kylie Smile – The treatment for cancer is cruel and terrible, but there is no other way at present. If we can do anything to help Kylie smile today and reach tomorrow, that is one day closer to the day we hear her declared cancer-free.

3. To make others Smile – There are so many children facing the same ugly cancer treatment as Kylie, she feels it is important to come alongside them and offer help and encouragement where she can.

4. To find a better way – For the rest of our days, Kylie and family will support research that offers a better treatment and end to this scourge of childhood cancer.

With all that in mind, our only politics are to support those who will vote to fund childhood cancer research. We do not hold to any party line. We will delete any discouraging or ugly remarks made towards those posting. This isn't that kind of site. Before you add something publicly, please consider that Kylie is only twelve, and we would like to be able to show her everything on her Facebook site, including comments.

In short, I don't care who you are, where you come from, what you believe, or how we are alike or different – if you smile for my daughter, solicit smiles for her, or follow her and care about her progress, you are my friend. I thank you and hold you in high regard.

So many people have sent gifts to Kylie. At first, it was hard to accept so much. Now we see that it does both Kylie and the giver good. Every smile, event, and big or little gift gives her something to look forward to and helps her get one day closer. We think it is important to thank everyone who sends something to Kylie. This has gotten hard lately. If you have sent something and haven't seen a thanks posted, I am sorry. Please contact me privately and I will rectify the situation.

* *Disappointment with God: Three Questions No One Asks Aloud*, Philip Yancey, Zondervan, 1992

When There is Nothing to Say

Maybe you have a friend dealing with a hard diagnosis or a life-threatening illness. I wrote the following three posts to share what meant the most to us when we were in the midst of our struggle. They have been picked up on various media outlets, and I hope they help others be the necessary and proper support for families suffering through tragedy.

What Not to Say When There is Nothing to Say

April 1, 2015

Recently, I was asked for advice about how to respond to the parents of a child diagnosed with cancer. Let me say from the outset that I am a dubious source whose council typically causes some manner of regret. However, since I have stood on the receiving end of some pretty stupid comments over the past year, I do have a fair amount of expertise in this particular area.

First, **THERE ARE NO MAGIC WORDS,** so don't try to find them. When one is at the start of a long, twisted road that includes the potential mortality of their child, words simply cannot soothe. They can, however, aggravate. So, I thought it might be helpful to look at some things that struck us the wrong way when we were facing our crisis.

What Not to Say...
When There is Nothing to Say

1. Do not equate anything you've gone through (or had a third cousin go through) with their situation. This is an immediate conversation ender. We once had someone compare a month-long sinus infection to Kylie's cancer.

2. One of the most frequent things we heard was, "What can I do?" No matter how sincere the offer, this can add stress to an already stressful situation. The parent of a recently diagnosed child has no idea what day it is or if they remembered to change their underwear for the past two weeks, so they will most likely have trouble assigning tasks to the three dozen people who have asked. Vague offers of help only muddle already murky waters.

3. By far the worst statement I got was, "I know how you feel." Uh, no you don't. Get back to me when you watch the rise and fall of your child's chest, wondering if it will stop during the night. And even if you have been there, your feelings and mine are totally different things.

4. Watch your quantity of words. Parents in this situation have a maximum amount they can absorb before they shut down. Docs usually fill that bucket daily.

5. Persistence can be irritating. There were weeks that passed when we just couldn't answer texts and emails. It didn't mean anything other than we were focused on greater issues. A second or third text reminding us of the original only made us feel bad for our inability to balance everything.

6. Don't expect to assume a role that you didn't have before diagnosis. If we haven't spoken in years, I likely have someone else to bare my soul to. It is fine to offer, especially if you have dealt with similar issues, but don't expect it.

7. Don't badger for information. We would have loved to have known specifics, time frames, and end dates. Unfortunately, these often don't exist in the cancer game and constant demands for information only serve to remind a parent of their helplessness.

8. If you made an offer that wasn't accepted, please understand it may be wanted or needed and simply came at the wrong time. Don't be offended or press for an answer. If the parent needs it, they will most likely return to it eventually.

9. "No" is a perfectly valid answer that people must be prepared to accept without justification or hurt feelings. The parents do not need added drama in their life and shouldn't be forced to manage the emotions of others.

10. With all of the fears and doubts of such a diagnosis swirling in the parent's mind, a mention of God's will can be a very slippery slope. While we are believers, religious platitudes were not extremely helpful, and I can only imagine how such words would be perceived by someone who isn't a believer.

This list is not exhaustive and I can only speak for my family. I think you will find it interesting that while we experienced all of the above, not a single cancer family ever did any of them. **Never.**

I would guess that this list could apply for other health or traumatic situations, but I can't speak to those since I have only navigated the pediatric cancer waters. (Look at me, trying to follow my own advice!)

.

What to Say When There is Nothing to Say

April 8, 2015

As a victim of a poor memory, I remember only flashes of our first weeks in the hospital. Visits, conversations, tears, rooms, tests, scans — they all run together in my cloudy mind. There is, however, one event I recall with perfect clarity.

He texted to ask if it was okay if he stopped in on his way home from work. I wasn't sure we needed a visitor, but Kylie agreed. Freshly diagnosed with Ewing's Sarcoma, we were in the pediatric cancer wing where Kylie had begun her first round of chemo. By the time he arrived, our patient was sleeping, and I got up to greet him quietly. I remember he put his backpack against the wall and opened his arms to hug me.

I am not a hugger…

    This is weird…

        He's here for Kylie, not me…

            Do I hafta??? Why????

                I'm okay, I don't need this…

Not a word was spoken and I promptly fell apart in his embrace. I cried like I had never cried in my life. He just held on for the ride.

What my friend Steve gave me that day was the very essence of what to say when there is nothing to say:

Love

Love is all there is. It can speak volumes without an audible syllable. It can be felt in a quiet room where words aren't welcome. It might be simplistic, but love is all that can break through the hard shell of pain and fear after a parent has heard the dreadful phrase, "your child has cancer."

Let me say again, there are no magic words that instantly sooth, but here are some things that resonated with me when Kylie was first diagnosed:

1. An expression of regret – "This really sucks" (or "stinks" for the less crass. But I assure you, it does suck!)

2. A profession of love and friendship. How do you say that? Um... *"I love you."* For those uncomfortable with the ever-personal "I," you can always lean on the family crutch for support and say, "We love you guys."

3. Presence. "I'm here." There are few positives in having a child with cancer, but one is that your calls rarely go to voicemail. Availability can be sensed. I knew very little in those traumatic first weeks, but I knew who was there for me, and I called on them when needed.

4. A promise of endurance. There is a long road ahead of the family. Like anything, many people with good intentions begin the fight full of fervor, but life gets in the way. No judgments here, I get that. A promise such as, "I am here today, tomorrow, and in six months," means a lot when given sincerely.

5. A *specific* offer of assistance. Sometimes, this isn't even verbal. If you see a need, meet it.

- We once came home to find a huge painted pot full of yellow flowers on our porch.

- Sometimes our lawn just got mowed.

- A woman who bakes incredible cookies would just stash dozens in our mailbox without a word.

- Friends organized meal calendars, ballet rides, and school carpools for our other daughters.

This is the action side of love. Love does! Love molds unique talents into lavish gifts. Doing love doesn't have to be grandiose or expensive and is often best when anonymous.

6. An assurance of prayer and/or positive thoughts. To know that my little girl was on the forefront of people's minds was huge. Knowing that children included Kylie in their nightly bedtime prayers was humbling – especially when my prayers couldn't get past a groan and balled fist.

What To Say...
When There is Nothing to Say

Nobody knows what to say to the parents of a child diagnosed with cancer. We didn't know what to say or what we wanted to hear – it was uncharted territory we'd rather not have explored. I assure you we were glad not to be travelling alone. If you have friends who find themselves on this heartbreaking voyage, I would urge you not to be afraid to approach them. Just step out in love, the right words will come. You might start with a silent hug. Even the bristliest of us cancer parents could use a hug from time to time.

How to Help When There is Nothing to Say

April 15, 2015

These final thoughts didn't necessarily fit under what to say or what not to say, but I think there is some worthwhile information that might help you tangibly support a friend whose child has been diagnosed with cancer and possibly other long term illnesses. I present them in no specific order:

Every child going through treatment for cancer should have an iPad. I know it sounds pretty crazy and so first-world, but I don't know how Kylie would have gotten through the boring days in the hospital without it. (Disclaimer: I do not work for Apple.)

Texting was the best way to ensure a message got to us. In the hospital, our phones were always on silent to help her rest and we rarely picked up a call. We both probably still have unheard voicemails from last April.

In the early days, we weren't very keen on surprise visits because Kylie's pain and sickness were extremely unpredictable. I'm sure that varies patient to patient, but we preferred a text first.

Help with siblings. This falls under the action part of love, but it spoke volumes to us in the early stages of diagnosis and treatment. It was so hard to balance our need to be with Kylie with the needs of her sisters. Friends grabbed them and took them to dinner, movies, and sleepovers. It was a great relief to know they were not only provided for, but having fun as well.

Most families going through treatment need some level of financial support or have a fear of fiscal unknown. If you can help, that takes an added pressure off. It doesn't seem like much, but a card with $20 in it makes you feel better when the rest of the mail is bills.

We were fortunate to have good insurance, but the costs that seemed to get very large were prescriptions and gas. If you prefer not to give cash, gas cards or gift cards to grocery stores with a pharmacy are particularly helpful. We also got a lot of restaurant gift cards, and they were wonderful to have on hand for our other children - who could use them when we had long days at the hospital.

There is a large community of support for children fighting cancer, and Kylie received things in the mail nearly every day. If your heart goes out to a cancer patient and you want to help, please understand that you will most likely never receive a thank you. We are good Southerners and it went against every bit of manners we've been taught, but we were just too overwhelmed to send out thank you cards.

We read everything – every note, letter, and comment on Caring Bridge, Facebook, and Instagram. I assure you that your words matter and comfort. Also, if you are letting kids send letters to a cancer patient, proof-read them first. Kylie got a couple from children who said things like, "It won't be so bad if you die because you'll be with Jesus." We knew they were sincerely hoping to comfort Kylie, but that was not what she needed to hear. We screened all her mail after that.

I hope some of this has been helpful. I know these don't pertain to every family or patient as I can only speak to our situation. We had incredible support throughout her treatment and we are grateful for it. I pray every family facing this long, terrible battle has friends to lean on. Some days, friendship and encouragement was the only way we made it through.

About the Author

Mark Myers lives in Georgia with his wife and daughters. He enjoys writing, running, building, and dreaming. In 2015 he lost his youngest daughter, Kylie, to cancer and is now a fierce childhood cancer advocate. If you would like to find out more about Kylie, please visit:

www.SmileyForKylie.com

www.facebook.com/SmileyForKylie

For more information on Mark and to contact, please visit his blog, *A Generous Helping of Laughter and Tears*.

www.MarkMyers.net

www.facebook.com/AGenerousHelping

Made in the USA
Middletown, DE
09 April 2016